The Gambling Times Guide To

Systems That Win

Volume Two

A GAMBLING TIMES BOOK

DISTRIBUTED BY
LYLE STUART
Secaucus, N.J.

THE GAMBLING TIMES GUIDE TO
SYSTEMS THAT WIN—Volume Two

ISBN: 0-89746-035-9

Distributed by Lyle Stuart, Inc.
Manufactured in the United States of America
Printed and Bound by Kingsport Press
First Printing—January 1984

Editor: *Jerrold Kazdoy*
Cover Design by Terry Robinson
Cover Illustration: Laurie Newell

All material presented in this book is offered as information to the reader. No inducement to gamble is intended or implied.

Other *Gambling Times* Books Available—Current Releases

(See page 164 for details.)

Poker Books

According to Doyle
by Doyle Brunson
Caro On Gambling by Mike Caro
Caro's Book of Tells by Mike Caro
The GT Official Rules of Poker
by Mike Caro
Poker For Women by Mike Caro
Poker Without Cards by Mike Caro
Win, Places and Pros
by Tex Sheahan

Blackjack Books

The Beginner's Guide to Winning Blackjack by Stanley Roberts
The GT Guide to Blackjack
by Stanley Roberts and others
Million Dollar Blackjack
by Ken Uston

Casino Games

The GT Guide to Casino Games
by Len Miller
The GT Guide to Craps
by N.B. Winkless, Jr.

General Interest Books

According to GT: The Rules of Gambling Games
by Stanley Roberts

The GT Guide to Gaming Around the World
The GT Guide to Systems That Win, Volume I
The GT Guide to Winning Systems, Volumes I and II
GT Presents Winning Systems and Methods, Volumes I and II
The Mathematics of Gambling
by Dr. Edward O. Thorp
Odds: Quick and Simple
by Mike Caro
P$yching Out Vegas
by Marvin Karlins, Ph.D.
Winning By Computer
by Dr. Donald Sullivan

Sports Betting Books

The GT Guide to Basketball Handicapping by Barbara Nathan
The GT Guide to Football Handicapping by Bob McCune
The GT Guide to Greyhound Racing by William E. McBride
The GT Guide to Harness Racing
by Igor Kusyshyn, Ph.D.,
Al Stanley and Sam Dragich
The GT Guide to Jai Alai
by William R. Keevers
The GT Guide to Thoroughbred Racing by R.G. Denis

The following *Gambling Times* books are scheduled for release in September 1984:

Poker Books

Caro's Poker Encyclopedia
by Mike Caro

Free Money: How to Win in the Cardrooms of California
by Michael Wiesenberg

New Poker Games
by Mike Caro

PROfile: The World's Greatest Poker Players
by Stuart Jacobs

The Railbird by Rex Jones

Tales Out of Tulsa
by Bobby Baldwin

World Class Poker, Play by Play by Mike Caro

General Interest Books

Caro On Computer Gambling
by Mike Caro

The Casinos of the Caribbean
by Stanley Roberts

The Casino Gourmet: Great Recipes from the Master Chefs of Las Vegas
by Stanley Roberts

The Casino Gourmet: Great Recipes from the Master Chefs of Atlantic City
by Stanley Roberts

The Casino Gourmet: Great Recipes from the Master Chefs of Reno/Lake Tahoe
by Stanley Roberts

The Casino Gourmet: Great Recipes from the Master Chefs of the Caribbean
by Stanley Roberts

The Casino Gourmet: Great Recipes from the Master Chefs of Europe
by Stanley Roberts

The Casino Gourmet: Great Recipes from the Master Chefs of the Orient
by Stanley Roberts

A Gambler's View of History
by Mike Caro

Gambling Greats: Profiles of the World's Greatest Gamblers by Pamela Shandel

The GT Quiz Book
by Mike Caro

How the Superstars Gamble
by Ron Delpit

How to Win at Gaming Tournaments by Haven Earle Haley

You're Comped: How to Be a Casino Guest by Len Miller

Sports Betting Books

Cramer on Harness Race Handicapping
by Mark Cramer

Cramer on Thoroughbred Handicapping
by Mark Cramer

Table of Contents

Part One
CASINO GAMES

WHAT YOU WILL FIND IN THIS SECTION

In the following pages, you will find some tried-and-true systems that win for blackjack, craps and progressive jackpot slot machines.

Part One
CASINO GAMES

3

BLACKJACK

In recent decades blackjack—or more properly twenty-one—has become one of the most popular games in casinos both in the United States and abroad. The principal reason for its popularity has no doubt been the growing realization that blackjack is the one casino game which, with intelligent play, can be beat. In fact, when a player employs a sound basic strategy, counts cards, and varies his bets properly, the odds shift away from the house in his favor.

When any game presents options for the player, the beginning of skillful decision-making moves exists. In the game of blackjack all of the options are open to the player, and none to the dealer. Therefore, it becomes a matter of the player making what should be the right decisions. Those decisions to be remembered come from case histories of situations for each of the many different types of hands that are dealt.

In this chapter, author Thomas Cate presents his system for developing expert blackjack strategy.

Chapter 1

The Chance-Skill Blackjack System

Expert Blackjack Strategy
in Three Easy Lessons

By Thomas Cate

I recognized that the non-professional weekend blackjack player is more interested in developing improved intuitive play than in learning the more complex counting techniques. I developed some training procedures that will greatly improve the playing skill of the typical part-time player.

My approach is consistent with many of the mathematically accurate counting systems. It is designed to help the player who has limited time to develop his blackjack playing skill. Also, these exercises can aid the advanced system player in developing the necessary skill to play under poor conditions, such as in a crowded, noisy casino.

Blackjack is a game of chance and skill. The odds are determined by the specific playing rules and dealing policies of a given casino; but individuals can develop playing skill. Books and schools which expose various playing systems are available. They are mathematically sound, but many part-time blackjack players have difficulty learning the more powerful systems.

Winning at blackjack takes a considerable amount of initiative, dedicated effort and training time. Few players have the opportunity to play regularly or to develop proficiency unless they live near a casino. A vast majority of players wish to play skillfully, perhaps once a month, but shortsightedly do not take time from their regular occupations to properly train for winning blackjack.

Women particularly seem averse to learning the card counting techniques necessary for winning and would rather play intuitively for fun. As one woman told me, "I believe you can win with your card counting system, but it takes all the fun out of it. It's too much like working." She plays for the excitement of the game; winning is secondary.

The advanced counting systems are most effective when played head-on with the dealer. Casinos, however, carefully limit the number of open tables. The $1 and $2 tables will generally be crowded at all times, while the $5 to $25 tables will tend to be less crowded. Unfortunately, the initial stake required for a good counting system is at least 100 times the minimum betting level.

Blackjack is a game of small percentage advantage. Even very powerful counting systems generally have less than a 3% advantage over the house. Many system players fail to realize that mathematically there is a real chance of incurring painful losing streaks in the short run.

Consider the odds in flipping a coin for heads or tails. While it is clearly 50/50, would you bet on having exactly 50 heads and 50 tails in 100 tosses of the coin? I hope not! Therefore, don't expect to profit exactly $3 out of each $100 played with a 3% system.

Unfortunately, the need for a stake of 100 times the minimum betting level ($200 at $2 table; $2,500 at the $25 table) means that most of us must play at the $2 tables. Accurate card counting becomes very difficult at a crowded table, yet the principles behind advanced system play can still be applied at the $2 tables.

The occasional player must often cope with erratic players, crowded tables and many other distractions. My recommendation for the occasional player is to first learn a basic-playing system, then alter it with intuition that is carefully developed through the following training exercises.

Basic Strategy

The occasional player must learn one of the basic-playing strategies before developing intuitive playing skill. The wide distribution of Ed Thorp's book, *Beat the Dealer*, served to educate most players with a basic system. To establish the basic system, extensive computer simulations were run which determined the best play assuming a normal deck.

The basic strategy must be adjusted to the specific casino rules. Reno and Tahoe casinos allow less options on doubling and splitting than Las Vegas casinos. This simplifies the basic strategy, but also shifts the odds against the player!

My basic strategy against the typical Tahoe casino is shown in Table 1-1. Pair splitting takes precedence if called for; then consider doubling. If you don't double or split, then play as a soft or hard hand. If a soft hand becomes hard after hitting, then play as a hard hand.

To learn the more difficult portions of the Table 1-1 chart, (such as proper play for the pair 9,9), I recommend practicing with a fixed 9,9 pair in your hand. Simply deal out the dealer's hand, (one card up and one down), then play according to the chart. Continue playing with an initial 9,9 pair for your hand. There could be hours of playing time between pairs of 9s in a regular blackjack game. This learning method is far more effective than just playing the game.

Understanding the Odds

To develop a winning intuition, we must first understand why the house consistently wins on the average. The house has one, and only one, real advantage over the player: *The player must assume the risk of drawing and busting before the dealer does.*

The player has the choice of drawing or standing, but will often be in a lose/lose situation. For example, if the player has a hard 16 and the dealer is showing a 10, the player is more likely to lose than to win, regardless of his skill. Skill can minimize losses in the situation of 16 versus a dealer's 10, but the player already risks more than the house before any playing occurs!

The other rules and options, such as doubling and splitting, when properly applied, are favorable to the player. Getting paid 1.5 to 1 for a natural blackjack is very favorable to the player and helps to offset the inherent house advantage.

To develop an intuitive feel for the game, let's consider what can

Table 1-1

BASIC STRATEGY — TAHOE RULES*

Dealer Shows:

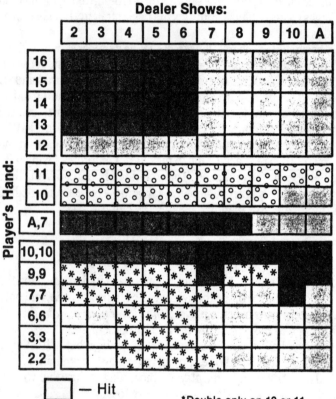

Player's Hand:	2	3	4	5	6	7	8	9	10	A
16	Stand	Stand	Stand	Stand	Stand	Hit	Hit	Hit	Hit	Hit
15	Stand	Stand	Stand	Stand	Stand	Hit	Hit	Hit	Hit	Hit
14	Stand	Stand	Stand	Stand	Stand	Hit	Hit	Hit	Hit	Hit
13	Stand	Stand	Stand	Stand	Stand	Hit	Hit	Hit	Hit	Hit
12	Hit	Hit	Stand	Stand	Stand	Hit	Hit	Hit	Hit	Hit
11	Double	Double	Double	Double	Double	Double	Double	Double	Double	Double
10	Double	Double	Double	Double	Double	Double	Double	Double	Hit	Hit
A,7	Stand	Stand	Stand	Stand	Stand	Stand	Stand	Hit	Hit	Hit
10,10	Stand	Stand	Stand	Stand	Stand	Stand	Stand	Stand	Stand	Stand
9,9	Split	Split	Split	Split	Split	Stand	Split	Split	Stand	Stand
7,7	Split	Split	Split	Split	Split	Split	Hit	Hit	Hit	Hit
6,6	Hit	Hit	Split	Split	Split	Hit	Hit	Hit	Hit	Hit
3,3	Hit	Hit	Split	Split	Split	Split	Hit	Hit	Hit	Hit
2,2	Hit	Hit	Split	Split	Split	Split	Hit	Hit	Hit	Hit

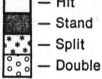

- — Hit
- — Stand
- — Split
- — Double

*Double only on 10 or 11.
Dealer hits soft 17.
No doubling after splitting.

Note:
1. Always split Aces and Eights.
2. Play 4,4 and 5,5 as hard hands.
3. Stand on A,8 or higher; hit A,6 or lower.

10

happen with hard hands of sums greater than 12 (excluding pairs, for now):

(1) Both player and dealer each receive hands of better than 17.

(2) The player gets 12 through 16, and the dealer's hand is between 12 and 16.

(3) The player gets 12 through 16, and the dealer's hand is 17 or greater.

The player has an advantage in the first situation because he's paid 1.5 to 1 on a natural blackjack and has even odds otherwise. It may not seem like even odds when you see a run of dealer luck: the dealer gets 18 to your 17, then 20 to your 19, and so forth.

Remember, if neither player nor dealer draws, then the house has no advantage. If there are aces left in the deck, then the player has an advantage over the house!

In the second situation, when both player and dealer initially have 12–16, the player is at a distinct disadvantage. The basic strategy generally calls for standing if the dealer has a low card showing (2,3,4,5 or 6) and hitting if he has a high card showing (7,8,9,10 or A).

In effect, we are playing as if the dealer has a 10 in the hole. All too often, the player will hit a 12–16 hand when the dealer shows 10 and a 2,3,4,5 or 6 in the hole.

Alternatively, the player may be standing on a 12–16 against a dealer's small-card only to find that the dealer has another small-card in the hole. For example, a 5 showing and 6 in the hole, (or 6 showing and 5 in the hole), particularly favor the dealer. You stood on 12–16 hoping the dealer would bust, yet he ends up drawing to an 11 with an excellent chance of making a good hand.

Other possibilities do exist, of course. Maybe both player and dealer will draw to 12–16 and have high hands without breaking 21.

Mathematically, the risk of playing first when you have 12,13,14,15, or 16 is high whether you stand or draw.

The third situation also favors the house. When the dealer has a 7,8,9,10 or A showing, the probability is high that the dealer will have a total of 17–21. Therefore, the basic system calls for drawing in this situation even though it is risky. The house has the advantage that the player will risk busting in order to reach 17. The player will break some

11

hands and lose some, while the house dodges the risk of drawing.

How can the player overcome the built-in house advantage? By using the basic strategy and making the best of all options, (double, split, insurance, and surrender if available), the player can almost have even odds in Las Vegas. Most blackjack authorities put the house advantage somewhere between zero to 1% depending on the casino rules and dealing policies. The player must religiously and accurately follow the appropriate basic strategy.

Basic strategy is fixed for a given set of casino rules and can be practiced alone. Simply deal two cards face up to yourself and two cards to a "dealer," one face up and one down. Play with Reno/Tahoe rules to the basic strategy in Table 1-1 even if you have to check out the dealer's hole card when an ace is showing. Since the dealer's play is set by the rules and your play is set by the basic system, you can practice by yourself (no fair cheating!).

While practicing the basic system, think about the playing options and probabilities. Suppose you hit a 12–16 hand versus a dealer's 10 and busted. Stop and see what would have happened had you elected to stand. Very often you would have lost with either play.

This phenomenon, and the small percentages that we deal with in blackjack probabilities, make it very difficult to learn the game by simply playing it. The best play for each given situation has been figured by computer simulation for a deck of normal mixture. This computed optimum play is the foundation for the basic strategy.

Card Counting

If you play enough hands, you might notice that sometimes a run of 10s occurs. The player and the dealer will tend to have high hands from these 10-rich decks. At other times, the deck will seem filled with low-value cards, and the dealer will hit hands in the 12–16 range with cards in the 2–7 range for very good totals (19,20 and 21).

As when flipping a coin, or in any other random event, there is a probability of various sequences appearing. The shuffle of the cards will occasionally result in a card sequence that seems abnormal from a blackjack player's viewpoint. The terms "10-rich" and "poor" are used to talk about these abnormal situations. The deck initially has 16 cards with a rank of 10. The probability of drawing a 10 out of a complete deck of 52 cards is 16/52, or 0.308. The ratio of 10s to non-10s is initially 16/36 or 0.44.

A 10-rich deck is one with an excess of 10-rank cards (K,Q,J,10). For example, about eight of the initial sixteen 10s are used by mid-deck on the average. The ratio of 10s to non-10s in the remainder of the deck determines the degree of "10-richness." A single deck with eight 10s and ten non-10 cards remaining would be a very 10-rich deck (8/26 would be normal).

The term "poor" means that the remainder of the deck contains disproportionate numbers of 2,3,4,5,6 and 7 value cards. The fours and fives are most important to the dealer. As a rough approximation, consider each four or five to be equivalent in importance to two of the 2,3,6 or 7 value cards.

The dealer is most vulnerable to a loss when drawing to hands in the 14–16 range. Yet, the four or five can turn these 14–16 losers into excellent hands. The 2,3,6 and 7 also help the dealer more than the player. The ace is unique in that it can be large (11) or small (1). The ace favors the player, particularly if the deck is 10-rich.

As you play, the deck will either muddle along in rough balance between rich and poor, or it will sway in favor of small-cards or 10s. The key to winning is betting high when the deck is rich and betting the minimum when the deck is poor.

In a single-deck game, the best opportunities will generally occur about mid-deck. At this point, enough cards have fallen to swing the deck significantly one way or the other.

The fewer the players the better. This is true because rich decks can be used before the dealer reaches you if you are playing in the seat on the dealer's right. Many players make their bets according to whether the dealer won or lost. This is erroneous. It is more effective to base your betting level on richness.

At first blush, it seems impossible to determine the ratio of 10s to small-cards in a real casino game. Remember, there are considerable gains to be made even from rough approximations. A number of clever counting systems have been developed to aid the player in determining a rich deck or a poor deck. Also, many players have sufficient "card sense" from playing bridge, poker, and other card games. Their card sense helps them estimate the richness of the deck as the cards fall.

I have found that learning a counting system and practicing it at home is excellent training for developing skills in estimating richness. There are many card counting methods available. These techniques are based on maintaining a running count that is roughly indicative of high-card richness relative to small-cards.

Most counts start at zero when the dealer has shuffled. For small cards played you generally add points. For 10-value cards, you generally subtract points. In some counts, certain cards are ignored, such as 7,8,9 or ace. In others, aces are counted as a minus value.

Also, most counts start at zero and would end at zero if the dealer deals all the way to the bottom of the deck. In between, the deck may stay positive all the way (high-card rich), negative all the way (poor), or it may fluctuate back and forth between positive and negative counts.

By now, some of you must be thinking: "This guy is nuts! How can you possibly count the blackjack value of your own hand, the dealer's hand, and then add this running card count for high-cards versus the small-cards?" It is difficult, but the secret is to count by combinations.

Cancel each small-card against a high-card then add up only the difference. For example, consider a hand where the dealer got 10, small, small and you busted with a 10, small, 10. Each 10-value card can be balanced off of a small-card for a net count of zero.

If instead, in a count where 8s were neutral, the hands had been four small cards, an 8 and 10, 10, you would cast out the 8. You would also cancel the two 10s against two of the small-cards, and then count the remaining small-cards "one, two" for a count of +2. In most systems, the running count is always a single number that is carried over from deal-to-deal until the deck is shuffled.

Even at crowded tables, you can estimate a rough count; simply cancel each 10 against a small-card and then count the difference. Of course, most card counters prefer to play head-on with the dealer. They can count much more precisely during the play of their hand since the dealer's hole card is the only unknown card that was played.

In card counting terminology, a deck is positive when the number of small-cards played exceeds the number of high-value cards played. The remainder of the deck will be 10-rich or A-10-rich by an amount equal to the value of the positive count. When the deck is positive, blackjacks and high hands are more likely to occur. The player will have better doubling and splitting opportunities.

A negative deck is one in which the number of aces and 10s that were played exceeds the number of small-cards played. When the deck turns negative, more stiffs will occur. The dealer will be less likely to break when hitting hands in the 12–16 range.

This suggests that the player should bet heavily when the deck is positive. He should bet the table minimum when the deck is negative.

A simple strategy is to bet a number of betting units equal to the positive count, but limited to a 4:1 spread. On a $2 table and a count of +4, you would bet $8. By keeping a running card count, you can actually predict "lucky streaks."

If a deck is very positive and the table is not crowded, then it will tend to stay positive through several hands. This gives the player an improved probability of a winning streak.

Once you learn a counting system, you will recognize whether the start of a winning streak is due to the card content or is simply a random variation with no particular likelihood of continuing. You will learn to parlay up on the positive decks, and to minimize the downside by reducing your bets to the minimal level on negative decks.

There's another factor to consider when card counting: the depth of play into the deck. The previously discussed card counts tell us the net number of high-cards relative to the small-cards, but we really need to know the ratio.

The probability of aces and 10s falling is our true concern. For example, an excess of four 10s or aces (+4 count), when most of the deck remains to be dealt, is not as prime as a count of +4 when only a small part of the deck remains. Four excess 10s or aces out of 13 cards is approximately twice as beneficial to the player as a situation where there are four extra 10s or aces out of 26 remaining cards.

This is precisely why casinos do not deal down to the bottom of the deck anymore. A good card counter can have a very large advantage near the end of the deck. To account for depth into the deck, the following technique is recommended for single-deck games:

(1) Consider the count to be correct at mid-deck.

(2) For the first one-fourth of the deck, multiply the count by one-half when you make your betting or playing decisions.

(3) For hands near three-fourths of the deck, multiply by two.

(4) In either case, don't use the adjusted number as you continue the cumulative count.

As an example, consider a deck that has a count of +4 after the first hand has been dealt. For betting purposes, treat it as a +2 count. When the next hand is dealt, return to the +4 count as your running number.

The approximating technique of multiplying by two or one-half may lack mathematical precision, but remember that there are gains to be made even from very rough numbers. The main point is whether the deck is positive or negative; the exact magnitude is not as important.

Developing Intuitive Winning Play

The basic system provides an approximately even game for the average deck. The real winning opportunities come from situations where the deck has become high-card rich and favors the player. To see this effect and to convert any skeptics, let's practice with a deliberately biased deck. Just remove these cards from an ordinary deck:

Ace-10-Rich Deck

Card Value	Remove
2	1
3	2
4	3
5	3
6	2

Total 12 removed
(count of +12!)

The remaining 40 cards will be high-card rich, and the deck will favor the player through all or at least most of the game. As before, deal one card down and one up for the dealer, then two to yourself. Bet aggressively and enjoy the game! Sure, you will lose some hands, but play through the deck (40 cards down to about 12) at least ten times.

Except for a phenomenal run of bad luck, your pile of chips will grow at an inspiring rate. The deck was started at a count of +12 and will probably remain positive. In a casino, you might have to play for several hours before getting to a deck this rich. Take advantage of it when you do!

Unfortunately, the deck is more likely to be poor than rich. To see the effect of a poor deck, start again with a 52-card deck and remove nine of the 10-ranked cards and three aces.

As before, there will be 40 cards remaining, but the deck is now very poor and is also ace-poor. This deck has a count of −13 in some counts. Bet the minimum and play through the deck at least ten times.

Unless you have a run of good luck, you will gradually lose on this negative deck. Both you and the dealer will usually draw, but you must draw first and will, therefore, break quite often.

By betting at a steady minimum level, the loss rate will be minimized as you suffer through this poor deck. The key in casino play is to plunge into betting only when the deck favors you, not the house.

Advanced Strategy

In playing through these biased partial decks, you may have questioned the basic strategy since it was designed around a normal, balanced deck. Most card counting systems include variations in playing strategy as a function of richness. To see the value of strategy variation, replay the previous exercises with the rich deck and poor deck, but incorporate some modifications to the basic strategy.

Rich Deck
(count of +4 or greater)
—Stand on hard 15 or 16 vs. dealer's 9,10, or ace.
—Stand on hard 12 vs. dealer's 2 or 3.
—Double 10 against dealer's 10 or ace.
—Stand on soft 18 vs. dealer's ace.
—Split 10s against dealer's 4,5 or 6.
—Take insurance when offered.
—Bet aggressively. A four-to-one ratio is recommended.

Poor Deck
(count of −5 or less)
—Hit with hard 12 or 13.
—Hit with hard 14 vs. dealer's 2 or 3.
—Don't double hard 11 against dealer's ace.
—Hit soft 18 vs. dealer's ace.
—Don't split aces against dealer's ace.
—Bet the minimum allowed.

I recommend practicing by yourself, or with a friend, until you know the basic strategy. Then practice with the two biased 40-card decks, both rich and poor. Use the minor variations in basic strategy. You will soon find that in actual casino play you will recognize when to bet aggressively and when to vary the basic strategy. Equally important, you will surely find some excuse to leave the table if the deck is low on 10s and aces.

Blackjack Terminology

BASIC STRATEGY—A computer-developed method for playing blackjack that may be easily memorized by a player without counting cards.

BLACKJACK—A popular betting game in which the bettor is dealt two cards, one face up and one face down; the dealer, too, has one face-up and one face-down card. The object of the game is to have cards totaling 21—or as close to 21 without going over, and coming closer to 21 than the dealer. A score of 21, when dealt an ace with a 10 or a picture card, is called "blackjack."

BREAKING HAND—A hand that will *break* (go over 21) with a one-card draw, such as a hard 12, 13, 14, 15 or 16. Also called a "stiff."

BURNED—Discarded; what is done with the top card after the deck is cut so that the player can't see its value.

BUSTED—To overdraw to a total greater than 21; an immediate losing hand.

COUNTING—The ability of a player to keep an accurate mental record of the cards that have been played. Can allow players to have a relatively good idea of which cards remain in the shoe.

DOUBLING DOWN—An option in which the player, feeling he has a good hand which will win with one more card, turns his two cards face up and adds to his bet by as much as his original bet. This gets him *one* additional card.

DRAW—To obtain additional cards to the original two cards.

FACE CARD—King, queen, jack.

FIRST BASE—The first seat at the blackjack table, immediately to the left of the dealer.

HARD COUNT—The true face value of the cards being played with.

HARD HAND—A hand without an ace, or one with an ace that can only be counted one way (for example, an ace, 6 and 9).

HIT—To add another card to a player's hand. The player asks the dealer for another card by saying or signaling, "hit me."

HOLE CARD—The dealer's face-down card.

INSURANCE—A side bet offered to the player by the house, when the dealer's face-up card is an ace, that the dealer has a 10 as his hole card, making blackjack. Pays 2 to 1.

MONEY MANAGEMENT—The manipulation of increments of one's bankroll in betting, the better to overcome adverse house percentages.

NATURAL—A total of 21 in only two cards. Automatic winner, pays 3 to 2.

PIT BOSS—The person in charge of the blackjack games.

PRESS—To increase the size of the subsequent wager.

PUSH—A tie between the dealer and player in which no money changes hands; a standoff.

SHOE—A dealing box for multiple-deck games.

SOFT HAND—A hand with an ace which can be counted as 11; like an ace and a 7, which can be counted as totaling 8 or 18.

SPLITTING PAIRS—An option the player has with two original cards of the same denomination (4s, 8s, etc.) of splitting the two cards and playing each hand individually.

STAND—What a player does when he is satisfied with his existing cards and stays with his hand as is.

SURRENDER—The ability of the player to give up only half his bet when the player believes he cannot beat the dealer. Must be done before any cards are drawn. Available only in certain casinos.

THIRD BASE—Last seat at the blackjack table, immediately to the right of the dealer.

TOKE—The tip or gratuity given to dealers from players.

"21"—Another name for the game of blackjack. Also, the winning total in blackjack.

UP CARD—The dealer's face-up card.

CRAPS

Craps has forever been an integral part of casino gambling. It's the kind of game that provides constant action and excitement. Standing around the dice table, players become involved physically in rolling the dice, placing their chips on the various proposition bets, picking up their winnings, and so on. Then, too, they're involved in voice and gesture, exhorting the dice to turn up a winner when they come to rest at the end of the green felt table.

There's no way of charting a pattern in craps. You learn nothing at all from any previous roll of the dice. It's all a matter of chance based upon the mathematical odds of any combination of numbers appearing on a given roll.

Accepting this irrefutable fact, it now becomes a matter of correct play. What are the best bets? How do you make the most money off of a roll? How can you lose less?

The answers to these questions are your keys to winning at craps. In this chapter, author Robert Eisenstadt presents his winning system for craps.

Chapter 2

The 31 Craps System

By Robert Eisenstadt

This chapter presents a comprehensive analysis of an ingenious craps system—the 31 system. Using this method, the player makes a sequence of line bets. Anytime he wins two bets in a row, he automatically shows a net profit for the sequence, and for any sequence, he has an 89.2 percent chance of making two consecutive wins. Yet the system is relatively conservative because the size of the bets is not huge.

In his book, *Your Best Bet,* Mike Goodman makes a cursory reference to the 31 system, which he says "has been played for over 50 years by hustlers and crossroaders around the country. . . It is one of the best and simplest systems. . . I knew one hustler who. . . left a small fortune for his widow, most of it won playing the 31 system. . . Because of that system, he never did a day's work in the 30 years he spent in Las Vegas."

I present the system here in detail. This chapter will be of value not only in shedding light on a unique system, but also in illustrating how any craps system can be and should be rigorously analyzed.

The tables, statistics, and most of the terminology and analyses presented here are of my own devising.

Terminology

Before setting out the specific rules of the 31 system, I will explain the system's general structure and some of its terminology.

The heart of the 31 system is to win two bets in a row after the loss of a one-unit bet.

The system consists of "bets," "betting plateaus," and "betting sequences":

(1) *Bets.* Using the 31 system, the player makes either all "pass line" bets or all "don't pass line" bets. For the uninitiated, these are the standard bets in craps. They are paid off at 1–1; that is, the bettor risks a certain number of betting units to win the same number of units.

Throughout this chapter and its tables, it is assumed (1) pass line bets are being wagered, and (2) $1 is the value of a betting unit.

(2) *Betting plateau.* As used here, "betting plateau 1" is the first bet of the system—the loss of one betting unit. Each of the following betting plateaus is merely an attempt to win two bets in a row. Therefore, each betting plateau (after the first plateau) has either one or two bets. If you lose the first bet of the plateau (the initial bet), that is the only bet of the plateau. But if you win the first bet of the plateau, you make a second wager (the double up bet).

(3) *Betting sequence.* A "sequence" is simply a chain of betting plateaus that is ended by either two consecutive wins or by the inability to win twice in a row given eight attempts to do so after the loss of one unit. Thus every sequence has a maximum of nine betting plateaus.

Rules of the 31 System

First Betting Plateau. The first bet is always $1. If you win, continue betting this amount. When you finally lose a $1 bet, advance to plateau 2.

Second to Eighth Betting Plateaus—For each of the second through eighth betting plateaus, you begin by making the initial bet of the plateau as listed in Table 2-1. If you lose the initial bet, advance to the next betting plateau. If you win the initial bet, make a double up bet (that is, bet double the amount of the initial wager). If you lose the double up bet, advance to the next betting plateau; if you win the double up bet, you automatically show a net profit for the sequence, and you end this series right there. If you wish to continue playing, you start a new sequence at bet 1 ($1).

Ninth Betting Plateau—If you reach the ninth betting plateau of a sequence, you bet $8. If you lose the $8 bet, you must end the sequence there, with a total loss of $31 for the sequence. If you win the

Table 2-1

The 31 System

Betting Plateau	(a) Amount of Initial Bet	(b) Amount of Double Up Bet	(c) Net Profit for Betting Plateau if Win Initial Bet and Double Up Bet (a) + (b)	(d) Cumulative Losses Prior to this Betting Plateau	(e) Net Profit for Sequence if Win Initial Bet and Double Up Bet (c) − (d)
1	$ 1	DNA*	DNA*	$0	DNA*
2	1	$2	$3	1	$2
3	1	2	3	2	1
4	2	4	6	3	3
5	2	4	6	5	1
6	4	8	12	7	5
7	4	8	12	11	1
8	8	16	24	15	9
9	8	16	24	23	1
Total	$31				

*DNA—Does Not Apply

$8 bet, you make a $16 wager (double up bet); if you lose the $16 bet, you must end the sequence there (you end up a $31 loser for the sequence). If you win the $16 bet, you must also end the sequence there (you gain $1 for the sequence). Regardless of the final outcome, you start a new sequence at bet 1 ($1) if you wish to continue playing.

To solidify the reader's understanding of the system's rules, here's a sequence that ended with two wins in a row at the sixth betting plateau:

Plateau 1: Sequence starts with loss of $1 bet.
Plateau 2: Bet $1. Lost. Net loss for betting plateau 2 is $1. Net loss for the sequence is $2 (bet 1 and bet 2).
Plateau 3: Bet $1. Won. Doubled-up (bet $2). Lost; net loss for betting plateau 3 is $1. Net loss for sequence is $3.
Plateau 4: Bet $2. Lost. Net loss for sequence is $5.
Plateau 5: Bet $2. Lost. Net loss for sequence is $7.
Plateau 6: Bet $4. Won. Doubled-up (bet $8). Won. Net gain for betting plateau 6 is $12 ($4 + $8 = $12). Net gain for sequence is $5 ($12 − $7 = $5). Stop sequence. Return to bet 1 ($1).

In this example, the player became a winner at betting plateau 6. This illustration should help you understand Table 2-1 more clearly. Go to Table 2-1 and look at betting plateau 6. Reading across that row shows the $4 initial bet, $8 double up bet, $12 betting plateau profit, $7 prior losses for the sequence (cumulative losses for betting plateaus 1 through 5), and the $5 net profit for the sequence.

General Features

A main feature of the 31 system is that whenever you obtain a net profit for the sequence, you end it immediately. If you want to continue playing, you start over again at bet 1 ($1). This is why, if you win the first bet, you keep betting $1 until you lose. The rationale is: why increase the bet if you are ahead? Be happy with winning even a little money. Don't "press" the winnings out of existence.

One ingenious part of the system is that whenever you win a bet (other than bet 1), you always double up on the next bet; if you win that double up wager, you are always ahead (show a net profit) for the sequence. Then you stop the sequence and return to bet 1 ($1). Column (e) of Table 2-1 shows what your net profit will be when you win two bets in a row at any betting plateau.

The system always begins with the loss of a $1 bet. Following this $1 loss, the player is given eight chances to win two consecutive wagers. As the player climbs from one betting plateau to another, he is always a net loser for the sequence until he wins twice in a row. He must be a net loser until then, for he has advanced to the next betting plateau by failing to win twice in a row at the earlier stage.

Winning two consecutive bets is not as difficult as it might appear at first glance. Given just one chance, a player would win twice in a row about 24 percent of the time; given eight chances, the feat is accomplished 89.2 percent of the time. The player actually shows a profit for 89.2 percent of the sequences with this system.

If he fails to win two bets in a row—given eight opportunities to do so—he ends up a $31 loser. This will happen 10.8 percent of the time. (Note that we lose exactly $31 regardless of how many times we double up and lose after an initial win; for example, if we bet $2 and lose, we are down $2; had we won the bet and then doubled up and lost, we are still down $2.)

The attractions of the 31 system are clear: the player risks relatively little money (31 betting units) in a lengthy sequence of bets in which he can win as much as nine betting units and has an 89.2 percent chance of showing a profit for any single betting sequence.

31 System vs. Martingale

The martingale is a well known and poorly regarded system whereby the bettor doubles up every time he loses a bet (see column (a) of Table 2-2). A major problem with the system is that if you lose many bets in a row, you will soon run out of capital or reach the maximum betting limit of the casino.

The 31 and martingale systems are similar in several ways: the systems go into operation after the loss of a $1 bet; doubling up is in-

Table 2-2

Comparison of Martingale and 31 System

	Martingale System			31 System		
	(a)	(b)	(c)	(d)	(e)	(f)
Bet #	$ Bet	Cumulative Loss if Lose All Bets	Chance of Losing All Bets After First Bet	$ Bet	Cumulative Loss if Lose All Bets	Chance of Never Winning 2 Bets in a Row After First Bet
1	$ 1	$ 1	—	$ 1	$ 1	—
2	2	3	1/1.97	1	2	1/1.3
3	4	7	1/3.9	1	3	1/1.7
4	8	15	1/7.7	2	5	1/2.3
5	16	31	1/15	2	7	1/3.0
6	32	63	1/30	4	11	1/4.0
7	64	127	1/59	4	15	1/5.3
8	128	255	1/116	8	23	1/7.0
9	256	511	1/229	8	31	1/9.3
	$511			$31		

Note: "Pass line" bets used in table.

volved; winning is more likely than losing during any one sequence; once a small profit is made, the player returns to the start of the sequence; and you are risking much to win a little.

Yet the 31 system has mitigated many of the unattractive features of the martingale (refer to Table 2-2):

(1) Over the course of nine betting plateaus, the 31 system risks 31 betting units. With the martingale, if you lose eight bets in a row after the first bet, you are down 511 betting units.

(2) Using the martingale, you double up after every loss. Using the 31 system, you double up after every other losing plateau. (You also double up after every winning bet, other than bet 1 ($1).)

(3) If you win in any sequence under the martingale, you win exactly one betting unit. If you win under the 31 system, you win from one to nine betting units per sequence.

(4) With the martingale, the chance of losing all eight bets after the first wager is .43 percent. With the 31 system, the chance of failing to win twice in a row, given eight attempts after the first bet, is approximately 11 percent. (Only in this respect is the martingale superior to the 31 system.)

House Advantage

Despite what Goodman implies about the 31 system, no craps system—including the "31"—can overcome the house advantage and show a net profit in the long run. This is true regardless of the combination, sequence and timing of bets, regardless of whether you double up when you are losing (hoping for your luck to "average out" *a la* the martingale system), and regardless of whether you double up when you are winning (hoping to "ride out" a streak *a la* the parlay system).

As noted previously, players using the 31 system make either all pass line bets (1.414 percent vigorish) or all don't pass line bets (1.403 percent vigorish). Free odds aside, these are the best bets a craps player can make. They afford the casino its smallest advantage. Consequently, the 31 system as a whole will yield the house the same small vigorish.

Most players are "right" bettors; therefore, throughout this chapter and its tables, pass line bets, with their attendant 1.414 percent vigorish, have been utilized.

Table 2-3 demonstrates the house edge faced by the 31 system in two ways. Column (c) shows that the expected loss is $0.245 per sequence, given a betting unit of $1. Column (d) shows that the typical sequence generates $17.32571 in action (this includes the expected amount of double up bets). Now, 1.414 percent of $17.32571 is $0.244986, which rounds off to the same $0.245 of column (c).

Table 2-3 does not include bet 1 because this wager is not a part of the system or sequence. The system starts only after a losing bet of $1, and that bet is called bet 1. So the loss of $1 at bet 1 is "given." It would be inaccurate to include bet 1 in Table 2-3, which shows the house advantage for a system that begins after the $1 loss of bet 1.

The remainder of this section explains the information contained in Table 2-3 and shows how some of the figures were calculated.

Column (a) of Table 2-3 shows how often a sequence will end at each betting plateau. It shows that the chance of winning two bets in a row at any betting plateau is 24 percent. Thus, 24 percent of the sequences will end at bet 2 (sequences always end at two wins in a row). Eighteen percent of the sequences end at bet 3; that is, 18 percent of the time, we both reach bet 3 and win twice in a row there. Three percent of the time, we reach betting plateau 9 and win twice in a row there. Three percent of the time we gain betting plateau 9 and fail to win twice in a row there. You will note the percentages decrease as we go down column (a). This is because the sequence of bets is more likely to end at an early betting plateau than at a later one; that is, the early betting plateaus have "first crack" at winning two consecutive wagers. Column (a) shows that in 89.2 percent of the sequence, we will win twice in a row and realize a net profit. However, 10.78 percent of the time, we will not win two in a row; in those instances, we will show a net loss for the sequence.

The calculations for column (a) begin with the casino advantage of 1.414 percent referred to above. The pass line bettor wins 49.293 percent of the time and loses 50.707 percent of the time. Each betting plateau after the first one gives us one chance to win twice in a row. We have just said that the pass line bettor loses the initial bet 50.707 percent of the time; when that happens, he cannot win twice in a row. But 49.293 percent of the time, he is still alive. He can make the dou-

Table 2-3

House Advantage in 31 System

Betting Plateau #	(a) Percentage Chance of Ending Sequence at Each Betting Plateau	(b) Net Units Won/ (Lost) at Each Betting Plateau	(c) Expectation of Gain/(Loss) (a) × (b)	(d) Betting Action
2*	24.2980	$ 3	$ .728940	$ .728940
3	18.3940	2	.367882	.857230
4	13.9247	4	.556988	1.297880
5	10.5413	2	.210826	1.332569
6	7.9799	6	.478794	1.752555
7	6.0410	2	.120820	1.727939
8	4.5731	10	.457310	2.160558
9—Winning	3.4620	2	.069240	2.095471
Total—Winning	89.2140		$ 2.990800	$11.953142
9—Losing	10.7860	(30)	(3.235800)	5.372568
Total	100.0000	(Net Loss)	$(.245000)	$17.325710
			House Vig.	× 1.414%
			Net Loss	$ .244986

*Note—Betting plateau 1 was intentionally omitted from table; see explanation in text.
Additional Note—"Pass line" bets are used in table.

33

ble up bet; he either wins it (49.293% × .49293% = 24.298%) or loses it (49.293% × .50707% = 24.995%). Here are the percentages for the average betting plateau:

50.707% — lose initial bet.
24.995% — win initial bet, but lose double up bet.
_____

75.702% — fail to win twice in a row; advance to next hitting plateau.

24.298% — win both initial bet and double up wager; end sequence
_____
100.000% — total.

Given two chances to win two in a row, the player will fail 57.308 percent of the time (75.702% × 75.702% = 57.308%). He will succeed 42.692% of the time (100% − 57.308% = 42.692%). That is, 42.692 percent of the time, he will win twice in a row at either betting plateau 2 or 3. We have already seen that 24.298 percent of the time, it happens at betting plateau 2, so it must occur 18.394 percent = 18.394%. 18.394 percent is the second figure of column (a). The third through eighth figures of column (a) are calculated in the same manner.

Given eight attempts to make two wins in a row, the player will fail 10.786 percent of the time (75.702% multiplied by itself eight times = 10.786%). He will succeed 89.214 percent of the time (100% − 10.786% = 89.214%). 89.214 percent is the ninth figure of column (a); 10.786 percent is the tenth figure.

Column (b) shows the units won at each betting plateau and the 30 units lost 10.786 percent of the time when we fail to win twice in a row after eight attempts. The figures in column (b) of Table 2-3 are simply those from column (e) of Table 2-1 increased by one unit. The reason for this has already been discussed. The system goes into effect after the loss of a bet. Thus, it is given that bet 1 ($1) is a loss. Column (e) of Table 2-1 includes this loss, but it would be unfair to include it in Table 2-3, which lists the house advantage.

Column (c) of Table 2-3 is calculated by multiplying the figures of column (a) by those of column (b). It shows the expected loss of the average sequence. Thus we have proved what was said earlier: 89.2 percent of the sequences result in wins, but the winnings are small; 10.8 percent of the sequences end with losses, but the losses are comparatively large.

Column (d). As mentioned previously, column (d) shows the dollar betting action generated by the 31 system when $1 is the betting unit. The individual figures of column (d) are the expected accumulated betting action of the sequences as they end at each betting plateau. It is interesting to see that almost 70 percent of the betting action occurs during winning sequences ($11.95 ÷ $17.33 = 69%). This is not surprising. We have said repeatedly that most of the time, we win with the 31 system, but we risk a lot to win a little.

It is small satisfaction that more of the betting action occurs at (a) than at (b). In the 31 system, the bettor, in effect, is laying the odds. He knows that all of his small wins can be more than wiped out by one untimely blow. He hopes to snatch a few victories while the gods of chance are napping.

I conclude this section with the following statistics of the 31 system, some of which have not been previously noted:

(1) One wins 89.2 percent of the sequences, winning one to nine betting units.

(2) One loses 10.8 percent of the sequences, always losing 31 betting units.

(3) Using pass line bets, the system affords the casino a 1.414 percent advantage.

(4) The average sequence ($1 betting unit):
   (a) Consists of 5.9 decisions (bets).
   (b) Generates $17.33 in betting action, $8.785 in losing bets, and $8.540 in winning bets.
   (c) Loses $0.245 (24.5 percent of a betting unit).

Postscript

The 31 system may be used for games other than craps. Playing craps, you may bet right or wrong. In the long run, the system can work when you take the free odds consistently. You can make the betting unit any amount, not just $1. As with any method, you can increase the value of the betting unit as you begin to win.

If you wish, you can extend the sequence past nine betting plateaus. You can make betting plateau 10, $16; 11, $16; 12, $32; 13, $32; 14, $64 and so on. This increases the probability of winning any sequence; it also heightens the severity of losing (never winning two bets in a row).

The 31 system can be modified along conservative lines. One approach, dubbed the "26 system," retains all the rules of the 31 system, but makes the initial bets of the nine plateaus 1, 1, 1, 2, 2, 3, 4, 5, and 7 betting units. Only 26 units are risked, and the player has the same 89.2 percent chance of winning, though he will gain only one to three units. An even more conservative approach makes the initial bets 1, 1, 1, 1, 2, 2, 3, 4, and 5 units. Only 20 units are risked in any sequence, and the player has an 89.2 percent chance of breaking even or winning one or two units. Because the system starts with the loss of one unit, breaking even is a minor accomplishment. These modifications are shown in Table 2-4.

You should decide in advance at what profit/loss level you will quit. As with all casino games (except blackjack), the odds favor the house. Enjoyment should be your main objective. In the short run, you are gambling that good luck will overcome the small house edge.

Table 2-4

Modifications of the 31 System

Betting Plateau #	Original 31 System		Conservative 26 System		Very Conservative 20 System	
	Initial Bet	Net Profit	Initial Bet	Net Profit	Initial Bet	Net Profit
1	$ 1	DNA*	$ 1	DNA*	$ 1	DNA*
2	1	$2	1	$2	1	$2
3	1	1	1	1	1	1
4	2	3	2	3	1	0
5	2	1	2	1	2	2
6	4	5	3	2	2	0
7	4	1	4	2	3	1
8	8	9	5	1	4	1
9	8	1	7	2	5	0
Totals	$31		$26		$20	

*DNA—Does Not Apply.

Note—"Net profit" figures are net profit for sequence when two wins in a row occur at respective betting plateau.

Craps Terminology

ANY CRAPS—A one-toss bet on all of the craps numbers with one unit, or group of units, bet on the 2, 3, 12. Payoff is 7 to 1.

ANY SEVEN—A one-toss bet on any of the possible combinations of 7. Payoff is 4 to 1.

BANKROLL—A player's total amount of betting money. Many players divide their bankrolls into smaller increments to extend their betting ability.

BARRED NUMBER—Can be either 2 or 12. Creates a *standoff* or *push* when betting *don't pass* or *don't come*. In a standoff or push, neither you nor the casino win any money; your bet is unaffected.

BET NUMBERS ACROSS—A group of five bets on all the place numbers *other than the point number*.

BIG 6 or BIG 8—A bet made on either 6 or 8 that it will be rolled before a 7 comes up. Pays 1 to 1.

BOX POINT—Shooter's number: 4,5,6,8,9, or 10.

BOXMAN—The casino employee who supervises the craps game and deposits money into the drop-box.

BUY BET—A place bet made at true odds rather than at place odds. Carries a 5% fee.

CHOP—A term which designates dice action of win-lose, win-lose, win-lose, etc.

COME BET—An even money bet. Exactly the same as a *pass line* bet, *after* the shooter's point is established.

COMEOUT ROLL—The shooter's initial throw of the dice after a *pass line* decision.

CRAPS—Common name for the game of dice. Also the name given to the toss of 2, 3, or 12.

CRAPS/ELEVEN—The name used to indicate bets in the specially marked area on either *any craps* or *eleven*.

DON'T COME—An even money bet. The same as *don't pass* bets, after the shooter's point is established.

DON'T PASS BET—An even money bet that the dice will lose, that a 2 or 3 will be rolled on the first roll, or that a 7 will come up before the shooter repeats his point. The same as *don't come,* except that the bet can be made only before a new shooter rolls.

DOUBLE ODDS—A bet permitted in some casinos in which the player takes an *odds bet* at twice his original wager on the line.

EASY NUMBER—Any even number that appears in any combination other than as an actual pair.

FIELD BET—A one-toss bet that 2,3,4,9,10,11 or 12 will be the next roll of the dice. (Some layouts use 5 instead of 9; some pay double or triple on either 2 or 12.)

FLAT BETS—The type of wagers in which the player bets the same amount on each roll, win or lose.

FREE ODDS—A bet on true odds permitted with *pass* and *come bets.*

FRONT LINE—The same as *pass line.*

FULL ODDS—The correct odds.

HARD NUMBER—An even number that appears exactly as a pair. Two 2s is known as *hard four.*

HARDWAY BETS—Bets made, in a specifically marked area, on an even number, that it will appear exactly as a pair. Payoffs are for greater amounts than if the number appeared as any other combination.

HIGH/LOW—A one-toss bet on both the 2 and the 12, with two units bet. Payoff is 30 to 1.

HIGH ROLLERS—Players who have relatively large amounts of money with which to play.

HORN BET—A four-unit bet that covers all three of the craps numbers (2,3,12) and also the 11.

HOT HAND—A succession of passes.

HOUSE—The casino; the management.

INSIDE BETS—A *place bet* on 5,6,8 and 9.

LAY BET—A *place bet* made that the shooter will toss a 7 before the number bet on. Player must wager more than he expects to win. A *lay bet* is a *don't place* bet at true odds.

LAY ODDS—An additional bet that allows the *don't pass* and *don't come* bettors to give, rather than take, true odds on their bets.

LAYOUT—The physical playing area in any game, usually printed on felt in the center of all tables.

NATURAL—A 7 or 11 on the comeout roll.

ODDS BET—An additional bet which can be made by players having *pass line, come, don't pass* or *don't come* bets, that the shooter will make his point. Paid at correct odds, or *full odds*.

OFF—A term indicating that bets are *not working*.

ON—A term indicating that bets *are working*.

ONE-ROLL BET—A bet decided on the next roll; as the *field*, 7, 11, or *any craps*.

OUTSIDE BETS—A *place* bet on 4,5,9 and 10.

PAIRINGS—The two numerals that come up together on a pair of dice.

PASS—A winning decision for *pass line* bettors.

PASS LINE BET—An even money bet that the dice will win either by coming up 7 or 11 on the first roll or by having the shooter's point repeat before a 7 is thrown. The same as a *come* bet, except that it can be made only before a new shooter rolls.

PERCENTAGE—In gambling, the hidden or direct charge made by the casino.

PIT BOSS—The supervisor of the gaming tables.

PLACE BETS—Numbered boxes in which the player wagers that any one of the numbers 4,5,6,8,9 or 10, will come up before a 7.

POINT NUMBER—In a comeout toss, the number that is other than 2,3,7,11 or 12. That number becomes the point number for every player on *pass* or *don't pass,* and remains until a decision is tossed.

PRESS UP—To add to the bet with winnings from the previous roll.

PROPOSITION BET—A one-toss bet on any of the three available craps numbers, the 7, the 11, or *any craps* (a combination of the three craps).

ROLL—To throw the dice; a throw of the dice.

SEVEN OUT—When a shooter throws a 7 and loses, after establishing a point.

SHOOTER—The player who is currently rolling the dice.

STICK—A curved stick, which looks like a hockey stick, used by the stickman to manipulate the dice.

STICKMAN—The dealer in the center of the craps table who uses the stick to control the dice action, and the pace of the game.

TABLE LIMITS—Smallest and largest bets permitted at the table.

THREE-WAY CRAPS—A one-toss bet on each of the three craps numbers, with three units bet. Payoff is as shown on the layout *for the number tossed.*

TOSS—A single throw of the dice.

UNIT—Any fixed quantity, when used in describing types of bets or systems.

VIGORISH—A 5% fee paid on a 4 or 10 *numbers* bet, which guarantees the player full 2 to 1 odds on the bet. Also refers to the house edge.

WORKING—A term used to imply that a bet is in full force and effect, even though the entire table may not be in effect at the time. Reverse is *not working,* which implies that for a given period of time the bet is *not* in full force and effect.

WRONG BETTOR—A person wagering that the dice lose; a *don't pass line* bettor.

SLOT MACHINES

The task of getting ahead of the progressive slot machines is not an easy one. As a matter of fact, most visitors to casinos, experienced players among them, consider the slots to be such a high risk, with a low probability of payoff, that they don't even bother with them! These much-maligned gaming devices have been nicknamed, as everyone knows, "one-armed bandits," referring to the ostensible hopelessness of any player leaving their midst in the black.

Not so fast! Although it is true that for most players—especially the inexperienced—the slots hold little opportunity for raking in a big win, in actuality there *are* ways to scientifically tackle the odds of those enigmatic spinning reels with their seemingly infinite number of combinations that can turn up on an evidently random basis.

In this chapter, author Victor C. Lingis presents his system for winning at the progressive jackpot slot machines.

Chapter 3

Progressive Jackpot Slot Machines

By Victor C. Lingis

It is often said that modern slot machines can't be beat; yet hoards of people, young and old, play them night and day for entertainment and fun. The fascination of the spinning reels and the jingle of the coins are hard to resist. In effect, slots are an adult's toy.

Maybe you don't believe in gambling on slots. What if you were offered to play the machines with somebody else's money? You'd get paid a few dollars for doing it, and maybe an extra $50 or $100 for hitting the big one.

It sounds impossible, but based on mathematics, it's being done indirectly and if you understood the mathematics of progressive jackpots, you'd earn those dollars. Unfortunately, the in-depth mathematical mystery which lurks behind the words "super-progressive jackpot" is one of the least understood features of slot machines. Don't worry though, this chapter will give you this expertise.

This chapter is not intended to encourage anyone to play the slots, but for those who do, your expenses can be kept to a minimum. I won't guarantee you'll always be a winner, but I will guarantee that, on the average, your cost per pull can be less over the long run.

Take stock of your financial position, and determine whether you will tackle the nickel, dime or quarter machines. I never fooled around with the dollar machines. The odds on them are difficult to calculate because of the IRS cut. The IRS will keep track of your wins, so it's up to you to keep a record of your wins and losses.

Let's establish the nickel as our basic coin unit. Dime and quarter equivalents can be calculated by multiplying by two and five respectively. The grind rate on a nickel machine will be about $25 an hour; on a dime machine it will be about $50 an hour; and on a quarter machine, it will come to a whopping $125 an hour. Players usually begin on the nickel machines and progress to the bigger slots after they have made a lucky hit.

There are several types of progressive jackpot machines: single and double registers, and three, four and five reels. Reading of the registers requires close study; pay attention to the decimal point, which is often hard to see.

To give you a better understanding, let me explain that the last two digits in the register indicate cents. All digits to the left of the decimal are whole numbers. Sometimes only three spaces are provided for whole numbers and when the pot reaches $999.99, a mechanic must reset the register to zero.

A mechanic installs a "1" to the left of the register to indicate that the jackpot is one thousand dollars plus the amount shown in the mechanical register. This prefix is altered whenever additional thousands are reached. Conspicuous placards indicate the location of the payoff line, the necessary symbols and the number of coins needed.

Most machines have two sets of lights which indicate that the player has inserted a sufficient amount of coins to qualify for the super-jackpot. You must make certain that these two sets of lights are working. *The casino pays off super-jackpots only if the proper lights are lit; nothing else counts!* One set of lights would be okay, but don't trust your luck to one system of lights. There is big money involved.

The thousand prefix may be made with a piece of masking tape. If you notice something to this effect, its validity should be confirmed with one of the change persons. (Any joker could install tape as a prank.)

Definitions

To understand each other better, I have established a set of definitions and assumptions.

(1) *Pay-outs*—The money which drops out of the machine into the money tray. Assume this money will go back into the machine.

(2) *Total money per pull*—The full quota of coins inserted needed to qualify for the super-jackpot.

(3) *Out-of-pocket cost per pull*—What each pull costs you. This will be less than the total cost per pull.

(4) *Grind Rate*—The per-hour investment it costs you to play the machine.

(5) *Go for broke*—Continuous play until you or your money give out, or until you hit the big one.

(6) *Break-even point or zero land*—The point at which your out-of-pocket investment is finally equal to the big jackpot.

(7) *Register*—The readout device on which the jackpot is registered.

(8) *Total money into the machine*—If the single jackpot is increasing at a 10% rate, then the total money is ten times what appears on the jackpot. On a double jackpot machine, the smaller pot multiplied by twenty will give you the total sum played into the machine since the last big hit. This total money, divided by total money per pull, will tell you how many times the handle has been pulled since the last big payoff.

(9) *Super-decal or super-symbol*—The symbol which determines the big jackpot payoff. Most often it is a big seven.

The Jackpot Register

The progressive jackpot represents more than just a plain set of numbers. It is a valuable source of important information. It is vital to make a written note of the jackpot size, the starting time and the starting bankroll before tackling a progressive jackpot machine.

To provide you with clues, take careful note of the following eight items that will be used in your calculations.

(1) *Progression rate*—On a single-register, determine the percentage the pot increases for each dollar inserted. On a double-jackpot machine, calculate the sum of the percentage increase with the total input inserted. Each pot should increase at an equal rate.

(2) *Total money paid in since last jackpot was hit.*—The house puts a small amount into the pot at the start of play. This can often be ignored, or just deduct fifty in your calculations. On a single-register

machine, the total money played in would be ten times that shown on the register. On a double-register slot, it would be 20 times the reading shown on the lesser jackpot.

(3) *Number of handle pulls since last jackpot payoff*—Take the total amount of money played in since the last hit, (preceding paragraph), and divide it by the total cost per pull of the handle.

(4) *Out-of-pocket cost per pull*—Assume machine pay-outs are fed back into the machine. Run the coin tray dry. Divide the out-of-pocket money played so far by the number of handle pulls since you started play. (Three hundred times out-of-pocket cost per pull.)

(5) *Your out-of-pocket grind rate per hour.* Three hundred pulls per hour.

(6) & (7) *Your out-of-pocket investment and the number of times you pulled the handle since you started to play:*

(a) On a single-register machine, deduct your start time reading of the register from the present reading. Multiply the answer by ten. This equals the total amount of money you inserted into the machine. Divide this by the total cost per pull.

(b) On a double-register machine, take the increase shown on one register, since you started play, and multiply it by twenty. The answer is the total amount you have inserted into the machine. Divide this total amount by the total cost per pull and you have the number of times you pulled the handle.

(8) *Gamble or odds rating of the machine*—The local people have a big advantage over the tourists. Locals can make frequent visits into town and watch the jackpots shape up. They can watch pros give up on a stubborn machine, leaving a big jackpot waiting for someone else. This isn't being greedy—it can happen to any of us.

If you found a jackpot which translated into better than even odds, would it be classified as gambling to play it? The pros know that a five-coin three-reel nickel machine with a single register usually hits between five hundred and eight hundred. A three-coin nickel slot hits between four hundred and six hundred. Both of these machines would be risky on a go-for-broke basis; but if you don't play them, someone else will.

Tourists have to take the best slots they can find and play them on a temporary basis. Jackpots occur in great numbers on weekends. The best time for scouting machines is late in the night or early in the morning.

The Gut Hunch

Many slot players are motivated by hunches. They have a strong feeling that the computers in the machines are programmed to hit certain combinations at reasonably equal intervals. Super-jackpots are frequently hit on the three-reelers but the odds are about 1 in 18,000. Progression is fastest on single-register machines.

Imagine we're looking at nickel, dime and quarter machines side by side. They are all identical single-register, five-coin, three-reel machines. The jackpots read $500, $1,000 and $2,500 respectively. At the 10% progression rate, they have had $5,000, $10,000 and $25,000 inserted into them, respectively, to reach the amounts shown in the registers.

Each handle has been pulled about 20,000 times (assuming most players, till now, inserted the full amount to qualify for the super-pot— about 95% do). At this point, the out-of-pocket input of all players is approximately 40% of the total input, or $2,000, $4,000 and $10,000 respectively.

These machines have reached only a fair stage for odds. If you were to play them continuously from this point, you would reach the break-even stage with about 6,650 more pulls on each machine. Your out-of-pocket cost for this many pulls would be about $665, $1,330 and $3,325 respectively. It would be quite a relief to break even, but is it good enough?

Suppose you came back a week later and found that those machines still haven't hit the jackpot. The pots are now $1,000, $2,000 and $5,000 respectively. Each handle has been pulled about 38,000 times or two full cycles odds-wise. They have reached a stage where many of the pros would consider tackling them on a long time basis because of competition.

The jackpots are ripe for the picking, but for the odds they are not yet even money bets. If you played them continuously from this point, you would break even after about 13,000 more pulls on each machine. The slots are overdue and your hunch is hard at work. If the three slots had pots of $1,400, $2,800 and $7,000 or better, they would all be approximately even money bets or better.

There is no guarantee that they will get that high or that they will be available at those settings. The grind rate and the general condition of the machines must also be considered.

For similar nickel, dime and quarter machines with single registers and the three reels, taking *three* coins per pull, the figures would be approximately 40% lower; the formulas would be much the same. For these machines the pots would read $300, $600 and $1,500 after 18,000 pulls. If played continually from this point, you would break even after 6,650 pulls (or thereabouts) as before. These machines would be considered ripe at $600, $1,200 and $3,000, but they still are not truly even bets considering the odds.

Figuring Out the Odds

The inside construction of slot machines is a closely guarded secret. From my observations and inquiries as an outsider, I concluded that the reels differ slightly as to the number of decals or symbols installed in them. I judge that it is within the range of 24 to 28.

For the purpose of this chapter, we will assume 26 decals per reel. Due to the many variables involved, 90% accuracy should be acceptable; and figures have been rounded-off.

To find the odds on a three-reel machine, we extend 26 to the third power, i.e., $26 \times 26 \times 26$ equals 17,576 or 18,000 in round numbers. If there is only one super-symbol per reel, the chances of getting all three lined up on the payoff line are 1 in 18,000.

In the case of a four-reel machine, we extend 26 to the fourth power, which is 456,976. The chances of lining up all four reels are about 1 in 500,000. On a five-reel slot, your odds are 26 to the fifth, or 11,882,000, or 1 chance in 12,000,000.

Once in a while on four- and five-reel slots, you may find an extra super-decal thrown in. While playing them, scrutinize the reels closely for decals; it will make a drastic difference in the odds.

In the case of a four-reel machine, with one extra super-decal, your odds of hitting would be $26 \times 26 \times 26 \times 13$. In this case, the odds are 1 in 228,444 or one-half of the original figure. With two extra decals the odds are $26 \times 26 \times 13 \times 13$, which equals 114,244, or half of the previous figure. Wherever a reel has two super-decals, substitute 13 for 26 in the equation.

If you pulled the handle an average of 300 times per hour, it would take 60 hours for 18,000 pulls. It would take 1,525 hours or 63 days to get in 457,000 pulls on a four-reel machine. It would take 40,000 hours or 1,666 days for 12,000,000 pulls on a five-reel machine.

These figures are all averages. You never know whether you're going to hit the lucky one early or late. That figure of 300 pulls per hour is fairly accurate. It takes into consideration time lost for lunch breaks, minor breakdowns, etc.

A Good Analogy

Let's digress for a moment and pick up a pair of dice. The chances of rolling a seven are one in six. Someone bets you $100 that you can't make a seven in six rolls. It's a fair bet; you accept and lose. Now he bets you $110 that you won't roll a seven in seven tries. You take him on and lose again. He offers you $120 that you can't do it in eight rolls. It's too good to pass up, but you lose again.

It's not unusual for dice to be rolled forty or fifty times without showing a seven. In this case, you couldn't ignore these good bets; at the same time, you didn't stand a chance to win back all of your losses.

It's much the same with a progressive jackpot machine. There often comes a point in time where the pot builds up to a value which is an even bet or better. A good example would be a three-reel, single-register, five-coin nickel machine with a jackpot of $1,400.

Should you decide to play this machine on a go-for-broke basis, you may have a streak of bad luck (again); there could be a point where the jackpot is exactly even with your out-of-pocket investment of $1,850 for 18,000 pulls of the handle. With 18,000 pulls at a quarter each (total input), your jackpot increases to $1,850 and you are at a break-even point.

Your odds have improved as in the case with the dice. Should you keep on trying and gain back some of your losses? It's an agonizing decision. (For a dime- or quarter-machine comparison, multiply these figures by two and five respectively.)

Double Jackpot Machines

Double progressive jackpot machines seem to be appearing in prolific numbers. It's easy to see why from a casino's point of view. When one pot is hit, there is always a sizable pot left to tempt the next player. The 10% progression is divided so that each pot increases at only a 5% rate, and it's to the player's disadvantage!

Quite often you will find a double jackpot machine in which the pot sizes are unequal. One might read $1,500 on one machine and $250 on another. Let's say this is a five-coin, three-reel nickel machine. There is a method to increase your chances of hitting the bigger jackpot if you are willing to sacrifice a smaller pot. Here's how:

(1) Get a supply of nickels, at least $10 worth. Make a note of both jackpot sizes at the start of your play. While carefully watching the lighted red arrow, start inserting five coins at a time in the usual way and pulling the handle.

(2) Watch the arrow closely each time you insert the coin. Watch for that moment when the lighted red arrow is on the larger jackpot just before you insert that first coin. If the arrow switches instantly to the small pot as you drop the first coin, put in one more coin and pull.

(3) Twice in succession, put in five coins and pull the handle. The arrow should point to the larger jackpot after those last two pulls.

(4) While watching the arrow, put in two coins again and pull; then five coins twice, each with pulls. Get the rhythm: five—pull, five—pull, two—pull; five—pull, five—pull, two—pull; etc.

If you lose the rhythm, then start over watching the arrow. Two out of three times you will try for the larger jackpot; the other pull will be a dud. It will take concentration to a certain extent until you get the hang of it.

This will change your average coins per pull from five to four. To figure your out-of-pocket cost per pull, run the coin tray dry. Check the jackpot increase by subtracting your starting time figure from the present final figure on one of the jackpots. Multiply your answer by twenty to get the total amount of money you inserted into the slot since you started to play. Multiply this dollar figure by five for your total number of pulls. Divide your personal money input by this number of pulls and you have your out-of-pocket cost per pull.

You can use much the same system for playing a three-coin machine. (These slots have jackpots that are imbalanced.) Your rhythm now would be 2-3-3-2-3-3-2, etc. For your total money calculations, you will be getting about eight pulls per dollar.

I've provided a chart which indicates coin rotation on three- and five-coin double jackpot machines. On these slots, the jackpots differ greatly (4 to 1, 5 to 1, 6 to 1, etc.). It is for players who want to better their chances of hitting the big one at the cost of sacrificing the small jackpot.

Assume that the lighted arrow normally switches after every two coins. It lands twice on the upper and twice on the lower register continuously in that order. The chart should work for any number of reels be it 3, 4 or 5. (See Figure 3-1.)

Useful Tips

If you are going to play the slots regularly, or go for broke, here are some tips to help you along:

(1) Have a strong paper or plastic shopping bag to carry supplies, i.e., your diary, pencil and paper, masking tape (to seal a coin slot at times), pocket computer, thermos bottle for coffee, and snacks.

(2) Hang the bag on the coin tray of your machine with a strong wire "S" hook. Keep your spare coins in this bag rather than in plain view where you have to worry about them. The change people often go off duty at night so you may want to stock up.

(3) If you see some pros playing a machine, engage them in a conversation and learn whatever you can. Study the quality of their machine. If the slots look good, find out how long they are going to play. You might make them a nominal money offer if they will save the machine for you in case they give up for any reason.

(4) If you are alone while playing, the change people will seal up

Figure 3-1

Five coin machine	Three coin machine
1 S	1 L
2 S pull handle	2 S pull handle
1 L	1 S
2 L	2 L
3 S	3 L pull handle
4 S	
5 L pull handle	1 S
	2 S
1 L	3 L pull handle
2 S	
3 S	1 L
4 L	2 S pull handle
5 L pull handle	
	1 S
1 S	2 L
2 S pull handle	3 L pull handle
1 L	1 S
2 L	2 S
3 S	3 L pull handle
4 S	
5 L pull handle	1 L
	2 S pull handle
1 L	
2 S	1 S
3 S	2 L
4 L	3 L pull handle
5 L pull handle	

"S" is arrow on small jackpot.
"L" is arrow on large jackpot.

Average four coins per pull; five pulls per dollar.	Average eight pulls per dollar.

Two out of three pulls will be for the larger pot.

and hold a machine for you while you take a lunch break or whatever. You will be asked to take all of your personal belongings with you, especially your money. Set a specific time. Tip the change people for any favors they do for you. And good luck!

Slot Machine Terminology

DPSM—Double Progressive Slot Machine. A slot machine with two progressive jackpots, a larger one and a smaller one, with a lit arrow that alternates between them as coins are dropped into the machine.

DECALS—The printed pictures of fruit, 7s, and other symbols on the reels of the slot machine.

JACKPOT—The highest prize to be won with the machine; usually, to obtain the jackpot, three bars or 7s must be lined up.

ONE-ARMED BANDIT—Slang term for slot machines.

PROGRESSIVE SLOTS—The type of slot machines which features jackpots that grow larger as more coins are fed into it.

SLOTS—Common vernacular for slot machines.

Part Two
HORSE RACING

WHAT YOU WILL FIND IN THIS SECTION

In the following pages, several expert horse race handicappers reveal their winning systems for cashing in at the track.

Part Two
HORSE RACING

Chapter 4

Dead Weight—How to Make it Work for You

By Conal Brady

Most horse racing fans would probably agree that weight is a major factor in handicapping. Few realize, however, that the type of weight carried can be more important than the amount.

There are two kinds of weight in racing: "live" and "dead." Live weight is the weight of the jockey. Dead weight is the lead attached to the saddle; track officials require certain horses to carry this extra weight to make the race more competitive.

Because dead weight is a greater burden to the horse than an equivalent amount of live weight, the pounds of lead a thoroughbred is forced to carry could spell the difference between a winner and an also-ran. That's because the dead weight sits in the small of the animal's back and acts as an artificial drag; the jockey is able to shift his weight throughout the race, adjusting his balance and center of gravity to help the horse attain maximum speed.

Incorporating a penalty for dead weight into your calculations will improve the quality of your handicapping. However, before you can apply that penalty effectively, you must first determine the live weight of each entry in the race.

Calculating Live Weights

The *Daily Racing Form* occasionally lists the names of the jockeys and their anticipated weights. Transfer this information to a chart of your own. Next, begin checking the daily overweights. An "overweight" rating means that the jockey cannot make the prescribed weight the horse is meant to carry in a given race. For example, suppose a horse is to carry 115 pounds. Laffit Pincay has the mount and weights 117 pounds with his saddle. Therefore, the horse would be listed as two pounds overweight; you would list Pincay as weighing 117 pounds in your jockey chart.

Do not confuse overweights with corrected weights. A corrected weight might occur because of a late jockey change. Imagine that an apprentice jockey was scheduled to ride a certain horse. At the last minute, he is excused and a regular jockey gets the mount. The horse loses his five-pound apprentice allowance and must ride with five pounds more than shown. That is a corrected weight change.

You can find the latest information on weights, late scratches, and jockey changes at the track blackboard, usually located at the back of the grandstand near the payoff windows. There is also a board in the infield that shows the latest changes for the upcoming race.

Make sure to use a pencil when listing your jockey weights, as you'll be continuing to make adjustments from day to day.

You now have the jockeys and their live weights. The next step is to establish penalties for the dead weight a horse must carry.

The Theory of Equivalents

Based on years of statistical research, I now believe that carrying four pounds of lead at a distance of six furlongs causes a loss in speed of one-fifth of a second.

Here's the step-by-step method:

(1) For calculating purposes, add a zero to all speed ratings, i.e., if a horse shows a speed rating of 87, make it 870.

(2) Penalize each horse for the amount of lead he must carry in the race. If a horse is carrying four pounds of lead at a mile-and-an-eighth, subtract 32 points (eight points per pound) from his speed rating at this distance.

(3) Credit the horse for the amount of lead he carried in his past performances. For instance, suppose in his last race at six furlongs, he had a speed rating of 87 or 870; he carried 120 pounds, of which 113 were live. He therefore carried seven pounds of dead weight. At six furlongs, that would total 28 points. Add this amount to his original total of 870, and his final rating would then be 898.

(4) If the race you are handicapping is a six- or six-and-a-half-furlong race, consider the horse's past performance only at these distances. If you are handicapping a 1-1/16-mile race, consider only the past performance at that length. This rule applies to races at all distances.

(5) If a horse has not run in the past 30 days, eliminate him. There's one exception: If he previously finished in the money after a 30-day layoff, do not eliminate him.

(6) If a horse's last race was run on a slow, muddy or heavy track, use the results from his most recent race for your calculations.

(7) Use the speed rating from the horse's best race (taking into account the amount of lead carried) within the last 90 days. Credit him for the lead he carried and total. Take the total for the present race, add it to the total of the past race, and divide by two. This will give you an average rating that measures both past and present. For example, in a six-furlong race, a horse shows an 870 speed rating carrying 120 pounds; his jockey weighs 113 pounds, so he must carry seven pounds of lead. Seven pounds of lead at four points per pound equals 28 points, so the rating of his last race was 870 plus 28, making a total of 898. Three weeks previous to his last race, he ran a six-furlong race with a speed rating of 880. He carried 122 pounds, but his jockey weighed only 106; therefore he had to carry 16 pounds of lead. At four pounds per point, that is a total of 64 points. His rating on the race he ran three weeks ago would be 880 plus 64 for a total of 944. Take this figure, add to it the figure of his current race (898), and you get a total of 1,842. Divide this figure by two, and you get a final speed rating of 921.

Picking Winners by Weight

Here's the procedure you should follow in arriving at your daily selections:

(1) Start with race #1 as shown in the *Daily Racing Form.* If the race is a six-furlong race, put a "4" just above the space that shows the race conditions. For other distances, use the appropriate number from the speed adjustment column of the chart. Usually, all the horses entered in a race cannot be listed in one column; therefore, over the second

column, add the same figure you had in the first one. This will help you avoid errors. Follow this procedure throughout the nine-race card.

(2) Refer to your list of jockeys and their respective weights. Set up your penalties for today's races, placing the resultant figure in the center of each horse's past performance. This is the number you subtract from the horse's best ratings of previous races (i.e., speed rating plus points for lead carried). Suppose that a horse went 1-1/16 miles with a package of 120 pounds. His jockey weighed 111 pounds, so the animal had to carry nine pounds of lead. Nine pounds of lead at seven points per pound equals 63 points. His speed rating was 830 plus 63, which equals 893. Subtracting his weight penalty in today's race gives you his final rating. You will note that in reviewing the speed ratings from past performances, you'll find quite often a horse with an 840 or an 850 speed rating ending up with a final rating less than a horse whose speed rating shows only 800 or 810. This is because horse #1 carried little or no lead while horse #2 had to carry a bundle.

For this system to work well, you must do two important things. First, keep jockey weights as up-to-date as possible, and second, be wary of any race in which you don't have sufficient background information on the horses. If you remember these few cautions and follow the other procedures carefully, your handicapping is bound to improve.

Figure 4-1

Speed-Distance Equivalents	
Distance	Speed Adjustment (Points Per Pound of Lead)
5 or 5½ furlongs	3
6	4
6½ or 7	5
1 mile	6
1-1/16	7
1-1/8	8
1-1/4 up	10

Chapter 5

Mathematical Handicapping

By R. G. Denis

Although handicapping and betting at the track can hardly be construed as investing, the underlying principles are quite similar. Common sense dictates that "investigating before investing" is a rule wisely applied to any transaction involving money. It is not necessary to violate a prudent axiom because one anticipates having fun for his money.

Despite the fun and excitement, it is still a business transaction when a bettor purchases a pari-mutuel ticket and hopes to profit. If he does not expect to profit, why would he wager?

The mathematical handicapping method seldom allows the bettor to buy a pari-mutuel ticket on a favorite. The method takes advantage of the crowd's mistakes. It eliminates the notion that a 2–1 favorite in an eight-, nine- or ten-horse field is worth even a two-dollar risk wager. It isn't that the bettor can't afford the two bucks, it's that he can't afford the principle at stake. No handicapper can violate sound principles and make a profit over the long run.

Handicapping is not a science. It is an instinct for predictability. It is based on mathematical data found in the thoroughbreds' past performance records, and in the *Daily Racing Form*. A knowledgeable handicapper uses this important data to make his predictions. The ability to correctly use this information will measure a bettor's success or failure at handicapping.

Total accuracy might be a challenging goal, but an impossible task. The handicapper's success, much like that of any stock market investor or analyst, is not measured by the number of winners vs. losers. It is measured by the bottom-line profit or loss.

As in any sport which deals with flesh and blood participants, there is last-minute information which is understandably denied the handicapper. Does the owner/trainer plan to go all-out with the horse? Is the animal in top condition? Has the trainer decided to use blinkers or a shadow-roll on an experimental basis? Will either enhance the chances of winning? Will the horse get out of the starting gate properly and will the jockey's riding strategy prove sensible?

Despite these and other unknown factors, it is still possible to handicap on a profitable bottom-line basis. To do this, the bettor must understand how, why and when to bet. It is not possible to profit by wagering recklessly on every race. There is money to be won or lost depending on one's betting habits.

How *not* to bet is more easily explained than the reverse. One of the most common errors occurs at the place and show windows. Most bettors assume that it is smart money to bet place or show, skip the win category, or bet place and show to back their choice for winning. Novice bettors, ignorant of mathematical handicapping, feel it is good strategy, or security, to back their horse with place and show.

The experienced handicappers do not use place/show betting for two reasons:

(1) Both place and show betting are blind bets, (payoff odds are not posted for these two separate pools of money). Most tote boards show only the amount of money wagered on each horse in these pools. (It would require a computer expert, operating between races, to determine the potential place or show payoff figures.) Not knowing these payoffs, place and show bettors make gross mistakes in thinking that they are protecting themselves.

Let's say a nine-dollar winner pays $3.60 to place after competing in a ten-horse field. Would a bettor willfully accept less than even money odds before the race on his place ticket? I doubt it. If those bets constitute insurance, then the premiums are vastly overpriced.

(2) Considering both the numerical odds and the reduced payoff possibilities accompanying these odds, backing a horse with place or show money is simply a luxury no handicapper can afford. Until the track will sell you a $2 place ticket for seventy-five cents or a $2 show ticket for a quarter, there is no logical reason for visiting the place/show windows.

Intelligent betting requires some restrictions, but they are quite reasonable. Never bet a race in which more than nine horses are running. If you are extremely patient and self-disciplined as a bettor, limit the field size to eight horses and you will improve your profitability. Remember, a smaller field does not necessarily dampen the chances for a healthy payoff figure.

It is not the number of horses entered in a race which dictates pari-mutuel odds—it is the amount of money that is bet on each horse. This amount is compared to the total win pool that increases or decreases the corresponding payoff. There are limits, however, to this statement: A five-horse field would not produce substantial odds in all probability; an eight-horse field limit will not adversely affect pari-mutuels.

A greater obstacle than unknown variables is the number of horses per race. The presence of each horse reduces your chances for cashing a win ticket. Their numbers create hazards in the form of interference, crowding, falling and unruly behavior at the gate, possibly disturbing other horses.

The bettor's greatest aid is the tote board, assuming the odds do not drastically change just prior to post time. The tote board's numerical odds represent the size of the field. By using this, a selective handicapper can cash-in win tickets.

You can cut the numerical odds without affecting tote board odds. In fact, you could bet every horse in the field and totally eliminate numerical odds. With the exception of occasional long shots, this strategy would not produce bottom-line profits. By cutting numerical odds to a point equal with or lower than tote board odds of your betting choices, the quality of your handicapping will improve.

The best way to cut numerical odds, relative to the potential dollar return, is to bet two different horses in the same race to win. Using the eight-horse field as an example, there would be six opponents for your two selections, making the numerical odds 3–1.

In a nine-horse field, the numerical odds would be 3½–1, expressed on the tote board as 7–2. The larger the field, the higher the numerical odds. (Again, I advise you to limit your betting to smaller fields.) Once you have selected your two win candidates, it is imperative that the tote board odds for both selections be equal to or greater than the respective numerical odds. This situation gives the handicapper a mathematical advantage which no other system offers.

Remember, in an eight-horse field, both win selections must be quoted at 3–1 (numerical odds) or higher on the tote board. Otherwise, skip that race and begin handicapping the next race. There will be a few races in which the bettor must try his patience and discipline and refrain from wagering.

As the Figure 5-1 chart indicates, the more horses running, the more difficult it is to achieve a desirable comparison between numerical odds and tote board odds. What the bettor desires is a mismatch (in his favor) between these two sets of odds. The numerical odds versus tote board odds determine the "when-to-bet" phase relative to successful handicapping.

Figure 5-1

Size of Field	Numerical Odds With Two-Win Bet
6	2–1
7	5–2
8	3–1
9	7–2
10	4–1

To determine the two horses most likely to win any race, the best handicapping tool available is offered by the *Daily Racing Form's* speed ratings. Speed ratings are somewhat misnamed, since the figures include more than sheer speed. These ratings indicate how the horse handled the track's surface, whether he drifted, if he had enough heart to duel successfully in a stretch run, and, if he failed to win, how badly or narrowly he was beaten. He could lose by ten lengths to another horse who ran the distance in super-fast time, and still achieve an above-average speed rating.

Like any other statistic, these ratings will prove to be reasonably accurate when used properly. They cannot be used with any degree of success unless they are compared to similar track conditions. Incidentally, these ratings change from race to race. The handicapper must allow for a degree of condition variance for the horse by using more than just the most recent rating. In the *Racing Form,* use the past three ratings on fast track conditions only; skip over any rating on good, slow, sloppy or muddy tracks.

It is sometimes necessary to go back three or four months to obtain these ratings. Add the total of the three performances and write this figure beside the horse's name in either the *Form* or track program.

Once this process has been repeated for every horse in the race, select the two horses with the highest total. Should there be a tie, select the one with the least assigned weight. You will discover that most claimers have speed ratings between 50–75. Horses in the allowance and stakes class are most often rated between 75–100.

Once the two win selections are made, the tote board odds and the field size will determine whether you can afford to bet these selections. If the field size indicates at least 7–2 odds or higher on both win choices, then the corresponding tote board odds for both choices must not be less than those figures. Otherwise, you will have a mismatch in favor of the track.

Bet only one of your two selections, even if the tote board odds are higher for one horse. You are selecting two horses to win to cut the numerical odds to reasonable proportions. You must bet only those races in which both horses qualify. Do not vary the amount of your bet; stick with a constant dollar figure, or your bottom-line profit will be effected.

With proper selectivity, a fair amount of patience, and the will to profit through self-discipline, you can acquire a reasonable profit via mathematical handicapping. The method used guarantees the bettor that the risk-reward ratio is within bounds of mathematical respectability.

In conclusion, the old adage that "you can't beat the track" is correct. All racetracks take 16%–18% of the mutuel handle, and the state gets the largest proportion. The handicapper's opponent is not the track; it is other bettors. The remaining 82%–84% of the track's handle is up for grabs. The handicapper with the most knowledge can get more than his share.

Chapter 6

You Don't Have to Lose at the Races

By Larry Humber

You say you're a horse player. Having any luck? Or should I have asked?

I'd gamble that as an average racegoer you haven't the slightest notion of the realities of horse betting. You know very little about the percentages, and your expectations are more than likely totally unfounded.

Though you claim that you're out to make a buck, you know full well you'll be at the mercy of the pari-mutuel clerks the moment you arrive at the track. Though you make one mistake after another, you talk only of "stiffs" and "racing luck."

You want action, so you don't hesitate to take a flier on the daily double. You might grab the first half, but that's as far as it goes. Now you have some catching up to do.

There's a horse at odds of 4–1 that looks promising in the next race, the first exacta feature. Sure enough, it's first under the wire. Regrettably, the average player is apt to have coupled the winner with a 15–1 shot that doesn't run a lick. Now you're really in the hole. Though you usually disdain the "chalk" horse, you decide to play it safe and back the 8–5 favorite in the fourth. Who'd believe it—a no-good at odds of 25–1; the same bag of bones you bet on a week or two previously now gets up to win, nosing out the people's choice.

As your bankroll is now all but exhausted, you proceed to stab at one long shot after another for the remainder of the afternoon. Your only regret is that you haven't a single dollar left to wager on the day's finale, the trifecta. So goes a day at the races for the vast majority of bettors.

Yet, it was a very ordinary afternoon. Three of the nine winners were favorites, two were second choices, another was third favorite and the rest were long shots. Incidentally, any horse paying better than 5–1 odds ought to be considered a long shot. Some bettors are of the opinion that the long shots start at $50. You'd do well not to count yourself among them, as I'll explain later.

Smart players had themselves a whale of a afternoon. They knew all along that the chalk horse is always the one to beat and that second and third favorites should never be overlooked. Six of the nine races were won by the first three choices.

It's time that we looked at the percentages that govern the sport. Many people know that the favorite will win once in three races. What about the chances of the second and third favorites? What about that 25–1 shot? Obviously, a horse is more likely to place or show than it is to win, but how much more likely?

Second favorites will win one race in five; third favorites will win about one in six and a half races. Favorites will place every other race, something that gimmick bettors should consider. Furthermore, they'll show twice as often as they'll win, or approximately two races in three.

Incidentally, horses at odds greater than 20–1 will win about one race in 50. Think about that the next time you approach the betting windows intending to back a long shot.

Of even greater interest is the odds-on favorite. Horses at less than even money will finish first in nearly half their starts. Yet the majority of bettors ignore these odds-on favorites, hoping to come up with a winner from what's left.

What's the best of all? No, it's not that 12–1 shot that just failed to get up a week or so ago. The best bet is a horse that has odds of 1–9—the lowest track odds. Why?

Racetracks are required by law to pay ten cents in winnings for every two dollars wagered, whether it's to win, place or show. Even if you back the meet's most prohibitive favorite, you're guaranteed a return of $2.10 for every deuce you invest. That's to say it is worth 1/20th of your stake. In other words, a horse at the odds of 1–9 should reward its backers 19 times in 20.

Such an animal, however, is apt to pay off 29 times in 30, even 49 in 50. Be assured, you're getting the best of things, so don't fret about receiving a dime a deuce. At worst, the track take-out is reduced to almost nothing, and how often are you allowed a free bet in anything?

You ought to have guessed by now that the track take-out, *your percentage loss*, is not the same for all horses. This was shown by Tom Ainslie, the author of several best-selling books on race horse handicapping. Ainslie discovered that the "bite" is significantly larger for higher-odds horses and much smaller for lower-odds horses.

He found that a little over a nickel for every buck you bet would be given away if you stuck to horses with odds of 2-1 or less. Conversely, supporting horses at odds of 20-1 or more will cost you ten times as much, or over fifty cents per dollar wagered. According to Ainslie, any horse whose odds exceed 5-1 should be avoided. Those who still need to be convinced that low-priced horses are a bettor's bread and butter should read on. The rest may wish to skip the next few paragraphs.

Though the average race card has eight to ten races, let's trim it down to three for illustration purposes. In this case, the following results can be anticipated:

(1) Favorites will win one race;
(2) Second and third favorites combined will win one race;
(3) The others will win one race.

Your first reaction is likely to be, "See, the chalks are a losing proposition. They screw up twice as often as they succeed." I can't disagree, but let's take a closer look at these three categories.

If we assume that there are nine horses in an average race, there will be 27 horses in three races. Three of those 27 will be favorites, and six will be second and third favorites combined (there are 2 per race × 3 races = 6). This will leave a whopping 18 to be grouped as "others." Others include any horse not among the first three choices.

I've already noted that the favorite will win every third race. In other words, the top choice in any horse race has actually a 1-3 chance of winning. One horse in the next group will win, making any horse in that bunch a 6-1 chance. Finally, one horse in the third group will win.

As there are 18 horses in that cluster, however, the chances of one of them winning are only 1-18. Anybody who contends that it's easier to select a horse from the third group than from the first or second isn't playing with a full deck, or anything resembling one. A glance at the table in Figure 6-1 should clarify things.

Figure 6-1

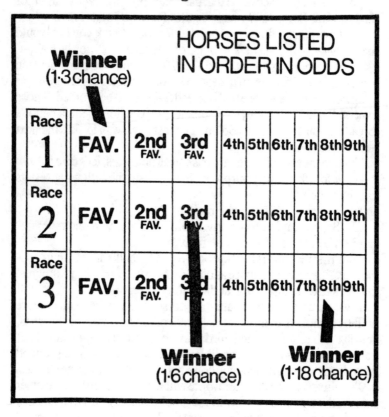

It should be noted that the chances of catching a long shot diminish as the field increases in size. If, for example, there are 14 horses to a race, the odds skyrocket to 1–33 for the third group. The odds on the favorite winning are still 1–3.

"Fine," you say, "but many times I've tossed out the favorite and gotten away with it." This brings to mind my next point: you don't have to wager on every race. That's another reason why the great majority of horse players are losers.

Always be selective—when you don't feel right about a race, don't risk your cash. Instead, pick the horse you think is most likely to win and jot down your proposed stake in your program.

Your choice will lose many more times than not, and you'll save as many dollars as you noted in your program. In effect, you'll be ahead that amount of money. You could go through a nine- or ten-race card and never pick a winner and not squander a single dollar.

Horse handicappers are an awfully suspicious bunch. They're convinced that, when their selection finishes out of the money, the animal was "stiffed." This is true especially if it's the betting favorite. That's to say, the horse was not supposed to win. Instead, it was manipulated in such a way as to prevent it from running first, second or third.

There's no denying that a great many races are fixed. For example, when a horse's odds are 4–5 on the board, yet looks hopeless in the racing papers, isn't it obvious that something is amiss?

Oddly enough, many handicapping books instruct us that the only horses worthy of play are those with 2–1 or 3–1 odds and turn up with 8–1 or 10–1 odds instead. Such an overlay victimized even Ainslie.

The point is this: when a horse is at substantially lower odds than it ought to be, go for it. Call it a fix, call it what you will. It's likely that you're looking at a winner—and looking at winners is what the game's all about.

Of course, the best horse doesn't always win the race. Those who suppose that the most likely animal will win every time are wrong. My findings suggest that there are roughly three of every four races (75%) which will be won by the best horse. There are even occasions when the favorite will win on luck alone.

Few bettors take the time to research current trends. For example, during some meets, favorites will win 40%–45% of all races. During other meets, favorites will be hard-pressed to hit 30%. Obviously, smart players will study these horses carefully while they race. Then, the next time their favorite races, they will bet.

I know of some high rollers who do very nicely by following the "hot chalks." Though the favorites may be slumping at one racing oval, they're apt to be next to unbeatable at another. A bettor must chart a number of tracks in order to take full advantage of this. The more you have to choose from, the more wagering opportunities you will have.

In the opening paragraphs of this chapter, I outlined a typical horse player's day at the races. I attempted to show you that a lack of knowledge about the realities of horse betting is a good way to lose money. Again, if your only ally is a substantial run of luck, you're invariably doomed to defeat.

Let's say our average player boasts a grubstake of $100. He's not looking to win $20–$30, or even $100. Rather, he's shooting for the moon—$2,000 to $4,000. He'll occasionally realize his goal, but for every time that he does, there'll be a half-dozen losing sessions. Simply stated, he's out of touch with reality.

This brings to mind my next point. In the long run, your winnings will be only a tiny fraction of the money you've invested; 5% is a considerable return, 10% may be unrealistic. If you wagered a total of $100, on an afternoon's card, you'd be doing well by winning $5–$10. To win $100, you'd have to risk as much as $2,000. Few players stake that much in a month, let alone an afternoon.

One of the worst things that may befall you at the racetrack is to select a $70 or $80 winner. Sounds ridiculous, doesn't it? You see, if you are successful with such a horse, you're apt to get carried away in subsequent races. You'll so seldom catch a big-paying winner that it's very conceivable you'll give back a great deal more than you've won before you hook another. For that reason, avoid books and magazines that brag of high-priced horses. They're selling illusions and you don't need them.

It's for the same reason that I suggest you shun all gimmick bets: doubles, quinellas, exactas, trifectas, etc. Ainslie calls them "trick" bets. "They are strictly sucker bait," he adds. My point is this: the payoffs often are so large that they are likely to cause you to lose sight of the way things actually are. How's that, you ask?

I stated previously that the number of dollars you can expect to win at the races will be only a tiny fraction of those you've invested. A return of $40 to $50 (not to mention $500) on a $2 ticket is way out-of-whack with reality. As I said, 5%–10% is all you should expect to make.

Once you've tasted a high-paying exacta or two, however, it's unlikely that you'll be satisfied with backing horses at even money or 6–5. Smart players, who take the time to examine their choices, depend upon horses with similar odds for their sustenance.

I also mentioned that, with a few exceptions, players beat themselves. Those who back long shots and indulge in gimmick betting are apt to suffer through extended losing streaks. If you can maintain your composure while losing race after race, perhaps for weeks at a time, then go ahead and play the outsiders, not to forget the doubles, exactas, trifectas and the rest.

You'll never be out of money for too long a spell if you stick to low-priced horses. I'll say it again—they're the astute player's bread and butter. On the fingers of one hand, you can count the number of afternoons that the chalk horse will be shut out in a racing season.

How do you select the winners? For most players, that begins with the purchase of a *Daily Racing Form*. Even though the *Form* is crammed with data on each entrant, it doesn't appear to be of much assistance—witness all the long faces on the way home from the track. It's my contention that the average player would fare far better without one.

One thing the *Form* does is encourage players to bet on horses which they otherwise would overlook. It also encourages players to overstake an animal. A horse which looks like an easy winner on paper may not be the cinch it appears to be.

Think back to your first afternoons at the track. You were probably reasonably successful, which encouraged you to try your luck again. The *Form* was something you barely understood then. If a neighbor had one, you might have glanced at it briefly.

After a few more outings—some good and some not so good—your curiosity began to get the better of you. You wanted to know more, so you purchased your first *Form*. Since then, you've struggled to make a go of it, yet at no time did you suspect that the *Form* was the source of your undoing.

There is only one item every player must have: a race program, which is on sale at the track every day. First and foremost, the program will tell you which horse is which. It will also tell you the race distance, who's riding, who owns and trains each horse, the number of pounds each animal will carry, the kinds of shoes being worn and post positions. Also noted is the color, sex, age and breeding of each horse as well as any changes of equipment.

More than likely, there'll be a page with the latest jockey-trainer-owner standings. There might also be information on how the favorites are faring and figures for each starting position. Finally, most race programs list the previous day's workouts, which you won't find in the *Form* as it goes to press the night before.

You'll soon come to discover that the *Daily Racing Form* is over-rated as a selector's tool. The time you'll spend trying to locate a winner in the racing paper would be much better spent studying the odds board and watching the horses parade. You see, selecting race winners is not that difficult a feat. I'd go as far as to suggest that the more variables you employ in attempting to come up with a winner, the less successful you'll be.

For example, if you considered class consistency angles, form angles, repeat angles, favorite angles, speed angles, jockey angles, tote board angles, public selector angles, and arithmetical angles almost every horse would be ideal. What would you accomplish? Very little, obviously! Yet, those angles encompass most of the principles in horse race handicapping.

If most of what you've come to believe in is nonsense, is there anything positive to be said about selecting race winners? A few years ago there was a study done by one ingenious handicapper. He analyzed all of the variables that racegoers use to pick a potential winner. Nearly every factor had no relevance whatsoever. According to his study, the only worthy variable was the size of a horse's heart—its willingness to give its all in order to win.

Such information is only hinted at in the *Racing Form*. The best way to learn about horses is to watch them run. You'll quickly come to learn which horses have heart and which ones don't. You should concentrate on the horses which make a determined effort every time. Every track has a dozen or more of these animals.

If you've been attending a racetrack regularly you can probably name several such horses. In the future, make a point of being there when they run. When these horses are sent off at low odds, they will seldom disappoint you, though it's not often that they'll pay more than three or four-to-one.

You might wish to group the horses with heart into a stable of sorts. Pretend that they're yours and play them exclusively; eventually, you'll know their ins and outs and you'll be able to back them with considerable confidence. Though you won't share in the purse, your reward will be forthcoming at the cashier windows.

In summary, if your other systems have failed, try sticking to low-priced horses, don't expect too much and key in on animals with heart. One thing is for certain—you don't have to lose at the races.

Chapter 7

The Power Quotient Thoroughbred System

A Racing Method That Yields Daily Profits

By Bruce McClarren

Okay, handicapper, here's a question for you: Have you ever seen a racing method that showed a per-day profit for a full month? Probably not.

Here's another: Ever see a betting plan that allowed a handicapper to walk out of two racetracks every day, for a full month, with a pre-destined profit? That, I'd be willing to wager, is just about 100–1 against.

I'm about to outline a method that accomplished those tasks, and did it in an easy-to-use fashion.

The Power Quotient Plan

The "Power Quotient Method" (PQ) is a combination speed-class formula which should prove to be highly beneficial for any thoroughbred handicapper. It considers two important factors:

(1) A horse's last-race effort, with a primary dependence on that steed's speed rating.

(2) The horse's money-making ability.

In other words, speed plus class equals a highly potent combination.

The Speed Factor

This matter is easily determined: add together the horse's last race speed rating, and the track variant mark that existed in that race. For example, if a horse recorded an 82 speed rating, and the *Daily Racing Form's* variant mark was 22, you'd come up with a 104. For later

multiplication purposes, convert this to a decimal, or 1.04. Simple?
You bet.

Here are a few other examples:

Speed Rating & Variant	Conversion
78–11	.89
91–10	1.01
63–23	.86

Just remember to add the horse's last-race speed rating with the variant which existed, then change that sum to a decimal.

The Horse's Wage Scale

Many racing systems have been devised, and most have dealt with a horse's money-box (that area of the *Form* which appears in the upper right-hand corner of past performances). The information listed includes the thoroughbred's starts for the past two seasons, and the number of times it was able to run first, second or third. Finally, it offers the most cogent of information: The amount of money earned by the racer.

It will look something like this:

1980   21   3   3   3   30,965

The competitor started 21 times this season and won a trio of races, he finished second three other times, and picked up three other third-place finishes. He has earned $30,965 for his 21 efforts. The next step in the PQ process is simple: divide the competitor's starts into his total earnings. In this case, it's a mark of $1,474, or the average figure earned per start by the horse this season.

The PQ Process

Let's further assume that, in its last outing, the horse we've just examined had a speed rating of 81, and the track variant on that date was 23. Add those marks together and make the decimal conversion. Your answer should be 1.04 (81 + 23 converted). In the final PQ step, multiply the horse's speed figure by his average-earnings' mark. Once again, in our hypothetical example, we'd multiply $1,474 by 1.04. The answer: $1,523. (A race can be adequately handicapped in a matter of five minutes or less.)

An Example Race

To further analyze the plan, here's a pre-handicapped race:

No.	Total Starts	Earnings	Speed Variant	PQ
1	24	$9,424	85-20	411
2	20	8,315	82-20	423
3	6	1,200	84-19	206
4	17	9,990	83-18	592
5	10	7,280	83-18	735
6	27	5,400	90-07	208
7	0	0,000	00-00	000
8	19	8,477	92-15	477
9	19	9,015	90-10	474

The PQ selection is #5 with its 735 figure. Ironically, this is the system play, even though five other horses recorded higher speed ratings in their last starts. Also, others earned more money this season. That's where one of PQ's most potent factors comes to play; the rating attained by multiplying the horse's speed/variant rating by its average earnings reveals his true current ability.

The Tote Board as Money Manager

There are thousands and thousands of good thoroughbred handicappers. Their ranks become thin when you check their end-of-season profit figures. Unfortunately, for every 100 good handicappers, you'd hardly find three or four good money managers, and that's the second most valuable form of racetrack expertise. No matter how talented he may be at deciphering the myriad figures, which exist in the *Form*, no handicapper will have long-term success. He will once he learns to handle his betting intelligently.

Remember, for a full month the plan showed a profit each racing day at two eastern tracks. Well, one principal reason was a firm and intelligent money-management method to determine how much to bet on very strong PQ selections.

Determine how much a bettor wishes to win on a given race day. Keep in mind that the higher the mark, the bigger the starting bankroll. (That's not an opinion—it's a handicapping fact of life.)

Suppose a fan is walking away with $30 each time he visits the track. Here's how to use the tote board to handle the matter: The bettor chooses a PQ selection and, as post time nears, he sees the horse listed at 3–1 on the board. Since he wants to win $30, the amount to bet is established by the governing odds. Naturally, odds change as money is pumped through the windows, and it's difficult to estimate an exact figure for each race. For the most part, the board comes mighty close to winning pre-set goals.

Let's assume the PQ selection wins, and the bettor collects his money. Under this plan, he should call it a day. That's right. He didn't come to the track to bet every race and every gimmick, did he? If he did, wise money-management principles and he are rather incongruous allies, aren't they?

If PQ Loses

Suppose our handicapping friend happens to lose that first race. He still wants to win $30 for the day, but he is now down ten bucks. Obviously, in the next race, he'll try for a $40 score. Once again, he uses the tote board to decipher the amount bet on the second-race PQ selection. If that horse is listed at, let's say, 5–1, an $8 bet is in order. In other words, divide the equivalent odds to the dollar into the figure you wish to win.

Be wary, for the lower a horse's odds, the more the bet—and that can be sizeable, to say the least. For this reason, I suggest extreme caution if the want-to-win figure is climbing and PQ picks are near-chalk selections. In such a case, pass and await a horse whose odds allow a lesser amount to be wagered. But in the previously mentioned month-long tests, the outlined methods derived a pre-selection profit each race day at Belmont and Monmouth Parks. And no system I've studied has been able to state that.

Chapter 8

Blue Chip Investments in Horse Racing: An Update

By James McCleary

Gambling Times published an article in the January 1980 issue, entitled "Blue Chip Investments in Horse Racing." This article suggested a new approach to blue chip investments. The system involved betting only the cream of the nation's thoroughbreds in the best races available.

The wagering method was outlined in that article. It was predicated on the fact that most stables have a certain way to train their best horses. They prepare their horses for outstanding efforts in the prestigious guaranteed races which offer large purses to the winners.

In races where the purses are small or mediocre, a trainer will not always be "trying" with his charges. To the average racegoer, this would be betting on another "stiff." You can be sure, however, that this factor won't be working against a bettor during the $100,000 races.

The racing enthusiast can be confident that he will have an honest race for his money. He confines his betting action to the well-publicized, high-stakes races. This in itself will increase his profit probability as a by-product.

The concept, expressed as a formula, would be BH + BR = P, or translated: *Best Horses + Best Races = Profits.*

For the benefit of those readers who missed the original article, the rules for playing blue chip investments are:

(1) Consider only those races that are held at major North American tracks where the gross value of the race is $100,000 or more.

(2) A horse is eligible for consideration if it is the top consensus selection of the *Daily Racing Form.* Track conditions must remain

the same after the handicapper's selections have been made; if track conditions change, there is no bet.

(3) The horse selected must be the outstanding betting favorite just prior to the race.

(4) There can be no other co-favorite in the race (no other horse less than 3/1).

(5) Only stakes and futurity races are considered.

(6) There must be at least five starters.

Investments are made when all these conditions can be met. Each time a blue chip investment opportunity occurs, bet $200 across the board. During 1977, a total of 26 races qualified as blue chip investments and resulted in profits of $5,510 with across the board investments of those amounts. An update of the results of this system has been completed covering 1978 and 1979.

Playing only outstanding favorites in races worth over $100,000 will continue to produce favorable results. The results for 1978 and 1979 are:

1978 Results

Total win profits	$1,260
Total place profits	2,070
Total show profits	740
Total Profits	$4,070

1979 Results

Total win profits	$1,050
Total place profits	2,280
Total show profits	1,080
Total Profits	$4,410

A detailed breakdown of each payoff which produced these totals is shown on the accompanying charts (Figures 8–1 and 8–2).

An analysis of the results for 1978 and 1979 reveals a factor which could be put to profitable use by alert readers: *When betting this caliber of horses, place-betting produces consistently higher profits than win or show.*

One probable cause of this is the preponderance of win-betting on outstanding horses in these types of races. This throws normal payoff percentages out of line. Normal payoffs for even money favorites are: $4.00 win, $2.80 place, and $2.40 show. When favorites are bet down to less than even money, these normal payoffs no longer occur.

As most experienced players are well aware, there are many times when a well-played favorite will pay almost as much to place as to win. When these betting opportunities occur, the smart bettor knows the best bet is to place.

To emphasize this point, look at Santa Anita's San Antonio Stakes on February 18, 1979. . .

Tiller was the outstanding favorite at 3/5. When the gate opened, however, *Tiller* was knocked back and got off last. He was still dead-last at the half-mile pole. He began to rally at that point, was lucky to get through at the top of the stretch; he was just able to get up to win. The third horse was many lengths back.

Tiller's payoff: $3.20, $3.00 and $2.40. Anyone who saw this race, and had placed a large wager on *Tiller* to win, would agree that the smart bet was to place.

By taking advantage of this abnormal payoff factor and betting all $600 to place (instead of $200 across the board), a player would increase his profits by 50%. During 1978, betting in this manner would have increased profits from $4,070 to $6,210. During 1979, betting in a similar manner would have increased profits to $6,840.

Suppose you were to take a correlation between blue chip horses and blue chip stocks a bit further. You would bet correspondingly similar amounts to those invested in stocks and some very worthwhile profits could be realized. For example, a conservative average investment on the New York Stock Exchange is about $2,000. If a similar amount were bet on each of these blue chip horses to place, profits for each of the past two years would have exceeded $20,000!

Figure 8-1

SUMMARY OF $100,000 RACES ON MAJOR AMERICAN TRACKS DURING 1978
(Note: No Handicaps—Stakes and Futurities Only)

Date	Track	Race	Gross Value	Favorite	Odds	Results	Win	Payoffs Place	Show
14 Jan.	Calder	Tropical Park Derby	$122,000	Quadratic	even	2nd	—	$3.40	$2.60
15 Jan.	Santa Anita	San Fernando Stakes	$110,000	J.O. Tobin	3/10	2nd	—	2.40	2.10
28 Jan.	Hialeah	Challenge Cup Inv.	$100,000	Silver Series	even	2nd	—	2.80	2.40
12 Feb.	Santa Anita	La Canada Stakes	$110,000	Taisez Vous	2/5	Won	2.80	2.20	2.10
18 Feb.	Hialeah	Hialeah Turf Cup	$155,000	Noble Dancer II	even	Won	4.00	3.40	3.20
4 Mar.	Hialeah	Flamingo Stakes	$150,000	Alydar	4/5	Won	3.80	2.80	2.20
15 Mar.	Oaklawn	Magnolia Stakes	$110,000	Miss Baja	even	Won	4.20	2.60	2.40
19 Mar.	Fair Grounds	Louisiana Derby	$124,000	Quadratic	2/5	2nd	—	2.40	2.20
25 Mar.	Oaklawn	Fantasy Stakes	$129,000	Equanimity	2/1	Won	6.80	5.00	3.60
1 Apr.	Gulfstream	Florida Derby	$150,000	Alydar	1/5	Won	2.40	2.10	2.10
2 Apr.	Santa Anita	Santa Anita Derby	$195,000	Affirmed	2/5	Won	2.60	2.40	2.20
16 Apr.	Hollywood	Hollywood Derby	$284,000	Affirmed	3/10	Won	2.60	2.60	2.10
22 Apr.	Aqueduct	Wood Memorial	$109,000	Believe It	7/10	Won	3.40	2.80	2.20
27 Apr.	Keeneland	Blue Grass Stakes	$119,000	Alydar	1/10	Won	2.20	2.20	OUT
14 May	Hollywood	Californian Stakes	$214,000	J.O. Tobin	1/2	Won	3.00	2.80	2.10
17 Jun.	Woodbine	Canadian Oaks	$107,000	La Voyageuse (E)	1/10	Won	2.30	2.30	2.10
24 Jun.	Hollywood	Hollywood Oaks	$110,000	B. Thoughtful	1/2	Won	3.00	2.80	2.20
1 Jul.	Arlington	American Oaks	$113,000	Star De Naskra	2/1	2nd	—	3.80	2.80
8 Jul.	Ak-Sar-Ben	Omaha Gold Cup	$116,000	Grandeza	6/5	2nd	—	3.60	3.20

Figure 8-1, continued

Date	Track	Race	Gross Value	Favorite	Odds	Results	Win	Payoffs Place	Show
22 Jul.	Arlington	Arlington Classic	$105,000	Alydar	1/20	Won	2.10	2.10	OUT
27 Aug.	Longacres	Longacres Mile	$122,000	Bad'N Big	3/4	Won	3.50	3.00	2.80
2 Sep.	Ruidoso	Ruidoso Futurity	$127,000	Pocket Coin	3/10	Won	2.60	2.40	2.20
3 Sep.	Del Mar	Debutante Stakes	$122,000	Terlingua	1/10	Won	2.20	2.40	2.10
3 Sep.	Centennial	Gold Rush Futurity	$120,000	Native Rango	4/5	Won	3.60	2.40	2.20
4 Sep.	Arlington	Secretariat Stakes	$166,000	Mac Diarmida	3/5	Won	3.20	2.40	2.40
13 Sep.	Del Mar	Del Mar Futurity	$150,000	Flying Paster	3/10	Won	2.60	2.40	2.40
20 Sep.	Belmont	Matron Stakes	$104,000	Fall Aspen	1/20	Won	2.10	OUT	OUT
23 Sep.	Hawthorne	Hawthorne Derby	$122,000	Sensitive Prince	1/10	Won	2.20	2.20	2.10
7 Oct.	Keeneland	Breeders' Futurity	$141,000	Fuzzbuster	7/10	Out	—	—	—
14 Oct.	Keeneland	Alcibiades Stakes	$142,000	Terlingua	1/2	2nd	—	3.00	2.20
15 Oct.	Woodbine	Coronation Futurity	$145,000	MedailleD'or (E)	4/5	Won	3.60	4.00	2.60
19 Oct.	Meadowlands	Young America Stks.	$137,000	Spectacular Bid	3/10	Won	2.60	2.20	2.20
21 Oct.	Belmont	Turf Classic	$200,000	Waya	8/5	Won	5.20	2.60	2.20
21 Oct.	Keeneland	Spinster Stakes	$112,000	Pearl Necklace	4/5	Out	—	—	—
29 Oct.	Santa Anita	Norfolk Stakes	$198,000	Flying Paster	1/5	Won	2.40	2.20	2.10
2 Nov.	Meadowlands	Meadowlands Cup	$161,000	Dr. Patches	2/5	Won	2.80	2.40	2.20
5 Nov.	Santa Anita	Oak Tree Inv. Stks.	$150,000	Exceller	3/10	Won	2.60	2.60	2.10
11 Nov.	Keystone	Heritage Stakes	$100,000	Spectacular Bid	1/10	Won	2.20	2.20	2.10

	Win	Place	Show
Total $2.00 payoffs	$88.60	$94.70	$77.40
Total $2.00 bets	$76.00	$74.00	$70.00
Total $2.00 profits	$12.60	$20.70	$ 7.40

Total profits from investing $200.00 across the board:

Win $1,260.00
Place $2,070.00
Show .... $ 740.00
Total $4,070.00

Figure 8-2

SUMMARY OF $100,000 RACES ON MAJOR AMERICAN TRACKS DURING 1979
(Note: No Handicaps—Stakes and Futurities Only)

Date	Track	Race	Gross Value	Favorite	Odds	Results	Payoffs Win	Place	Show
20 Jan.	Santa Anita	San Fer. Stakes	$114,000	Affirmed	1/2	2nd		$2.40	$2.20
11 Feb.	Santa Anita	La Canada Stakes	$114,000	B. Thoughtful	6/5	Won	$4.40	2.80	2.60
18 Feb.	Santa Anita	San Antonio Stakes	$110,000	Tiller	3/5	Won	3.20	3.00	2.40
3 Mar.	Golden Gate	Calif. Derby	$150,000	Golden Act	3/2	2nd		3.60	2.80
6 Mar.	Gulfstream	Florida Derby	$200,000	Spect. Bid	1/20	Won	2.10	OUT	OUT
18 Mar.	Fair Groun.	Louisiana Derby	$157,000	Golden Act	even	Won	4.20	2.80	2.20
18 Mar.	Santa Anita	San L. Rey Stks.	$162,000	Exceller	9/10	Out			
24 Mar.	Hialeah	Flamingo Stks.	$149,000	Spect. Bid	1/20	Won	2.10	2.10	2.10
1 Apr.	Santa Anita	Santa Anita Dy.	$192,000	Flying Paster	3/5	Won	3.20	2.80	2.40
14 Apr.	Oaklawn	Arkansas Derby	$178,000	Golden Act	7/5	Won	4.80	3.60	3.00
14 Apr.	Hollywood	Hollywood Derby	$279,000	Flying Paster	1/5	Won	2.40	2.20	2.10
26 Apr.	Keeneland	Blue Grass Stks.	$121,000	Spect. Bid	1/20	Won	2.10	OUT	OUT
4 May	Churchill	Kentucky Oaks	$128,000	Davona Dale	2/5	Won	2.80	2.40	2.10
6 May	Sunland	R.A. Futurity	$267,000	Western Hand	1/2	Won	3.00	2.60	2.20
18 May	Pimlico	B.E. Susan Stks.	$111,000	Davona Dale	1/10	Won	2.20	2.10	2.10
19 May	Pimlico	Preakness Stakes	$235,000	Spect. Bid	1/10	Won	2.20	2.20	OUT
20 May	Hollywood	California Stakes	$272,000	Affirmed	3/10	Won	2.60	2.20	2.20
28 May	Keystone	Penna. Derby	$114,000	Smarten	3/10	Won	2.60	2.40	2.20
9 Jun.	Belmont	Belmont Stakes	$269,000	Spect. Bid	3/10	3rd			2.10
10 Jun.	Belmont	Mother Goose Stakes	$106,000	Davona Dale	1/5	Won	2.40	2.20	2.10
17 Jun.	Thistledown	Ohio Derby	$150,000	Smarten	9/10	Won	3.80	2.60	2.40
23 Jun.	Woodbine	Canadian Oaks	$109,000	Kamar	7/5	Won	4.80	4.30	2.80
24 Jun.	Hollywood	Hollywood Gold C.	$500,000	Affirmed	3/10	Won	2.60	2.20	2.10

Figure 8-2, continued

Date	Track	Race	Gross Value	Favorite	Odds	Results	Payoffs Win	Place	Show
30 Jun.	Belmont	C.C. American O.	$132,000	Davona Dale	1/10	Won	2.20	2.20	2.10
30 Jun.	Arlington	American Derby	$106,000	Smarten	1/20	Won	2.10	2.20	2.10
7 Jul.	Hollywood	Hollywood Oaks	$108,000	It's in the A.	even	2nd		2.80	2.40
14 Jul.	Hollywood	H. Lassie Stakes	$103,000	Table Hands	even	Won	4.00	2.60	2.20
11 Aug.	Saratoga	Alabama Stakes	$108,000	Davona Dale	3/10	2nd		2.20	2.10
2 Sep.	Centennial	G. Rush Futurity	$126,000	Broncomania	2/5	Won	2.80	3.00	2.40
2 Sep.	Centennial	G. Rush Futurity	$126,000	Silvers	1/2	Won	3.00	2.60	2.40
15 Sep.	Belmont	Futurity Stakes	$165,000	Rockhill Nat.	1/5	Won	2.40	2.40	2.10
8 Sep.	Belmont	Marlboro Cup	$300,000	Spect. Bid	1/2	Won	3.00	2.60	2.10
16 Sep.	Albuquerque	N. Mex. Futurity	$102,000	Banquero	2/5	Won	2.80	2.80	2.20
22 Sep.	Belmont	Woodward Stakes	$191,000	Affirmed	2/5	Won	2.80	2.60	2.10
24 Sep.	Belmont	Matron Stakes	$123,000	Royal Suite	2/5	2nd		2.40	2.10
13 Oct.	Woodbine	Coronation Fut.	$153,000	New Regent	1/2	2nd		2.70	2.30
14 Oct.	Belmont	Champagne Stks.	$136,000	Rockhill Nat.	1/5	2nd		2.40	2.10
18 Oct.	Meadowlands	Meadowlands Cup	$361,000	Spect. Bid	1/10	Won	2.20	2.20	2.10
20 Oct.	Santa Anita	Norfolk Stakes	$198,000	The Carpenter	1/2	Won	3.00	2.60	2.40
20 Oct.	Pimlico	Selima Stakes	$169,000	Smart Angle	1/2	Won	3.00	2.20	2.10
21 Oct.	Woodbine	Canadian Int. C.	$200,000	Golden Act	7/5	Won	4.60	2.90	2.50
27 Oct.	Woodbine	Cup & Saucer Stks.	$104,000	Allan Blue (Entry)	3/4	Won	3.50	2.50	2.40
27 Oct.	Pimlico	Laurel Futurity	$188,000	Gold Stage	2/1	2nd		3.80	2.80
3 Nov.	Meadowlands	Young America Stks.	$251,000	Gold Stage	6/5	2nd		3.00	2.60
10 Nov.	Bay Meadows	El Camino Real Stks.	$112,000	Doonesbury	7/5	2nd		3.40	2.80
11 Nov.	Aqueduct	Remsen Stakes	$107,000	Plugged Nickle	4/5	Won	3.60	2.60	2.40

	Win	Place	Show
Total $2.00 payoffs	$102.50	$110.80	$96.80
Total $2.00 bets	$92.00	$88.00	$86.00
Total $2.00 profits	$10.50	$22.80	$10.80

Total profits from investing $200.00 across the board:

Win	$1,050.00
Place	$2,280.00
Show	$1,080.00
Total	$4,410.00

Chapter 9

A Winner For All Tracks

By C.S. McCrary

Betty Grable had it in World War II, and *Spectacular Bid* has it today. It's called form, and it's a good bet either off or on the track.

Form as a selection method has had its ups and downs. It has varied as often as the length of women's skirts.

This method of handicapping has always selected winners, but there were usually two jokers in the deck. The first was the low mutuels paid for the winner and the second was the disproportionate length of time needed to find the true form horse in the race. It was possible to spend six or eight hours handicapping a race card and still end up with the "odds-on" favorite as your selection. You could have saved time by simply playing the consensus horse.

But who has time to waste? I certainly don't, and I suggest you don't either. What is needed is a fast, easy method of selection that will pick winners at prices worthy of your time and effort.

This system does exist, and it has worked at many tracks across the country. It picked winners at five different facilities, all on the same day. The tracks were Del Mar, Arlington Park, Bowie, Monmouth and Saratoga. The date was August 6, 1979, and the bets were laid at the Fremont Race Book in Las Vegas, Nevada.

Rather than begin with a long explanation, I will start by laying out the system so you can get to the track in time for the first race. You can read the explanations after the races are over and you have counted your profits for the third time to make sure you're not dreaming.

Here are the rules:

(A) Pick a horse that finished in the money at today's distance, preferably one that placed first. This race could be anywhere in the past performance; disregard all others.

(B) Your selection must have at least two of the following points in its favor. Bet on the horse with the most points.

1. Second-place finish in the last race.
2. Speed rating of at least 75 (and three points higher than the next-to-last race).
3. Four-year-old gelding that won its last race.
4. Finished in the money in either of its last two races.
5. Shows a workout within the last five days.
6. Won the next-to-last race or finished within one length of the winner.
7. Went off at odds in the last race that were the same or greater than those in the next-to-last race and did not win.
8. Won last race within seven days (or gained or led in the stretch last race).
9. Won last race or was within 12 lengths of the winner. Add the lengths beaten for the first call to the lengths beaten for the last call. Play the lowest number.
10. Finished in-the-money in the last race and dropped at least two pounds from that time.

(C) If your selections have the same number of points in their favor, pass the race. There are not enough dead heats to justify making multiple bets. Occasionally, the odds are great enough to warrant betting two horses in the race, but it is usually better to just skip the race.

You now have in your hands what I think is the deadliest handicapping method ever devised. It works on all kinds of tracks and races, though it is a good idea to avoid wagering on races run in the mud. It also works on maiden special weights, claimers and allowance races. It is also successful on handicaps and stakes events, but never bet them because the pari-mutuel prices are too low for these two races. Stick with the three-year-olds and up in maiden special weights, claimers and allowances; leave the two-year-olds, handicaps and stakes for those not interested in profit.

By picking a horse that has raced successfully at today's distance and has two of the ten points I have mentioned in his favor, you have a good chance of winning. You can't do much better than this system unless you use a gun at the cashier's window.

Here is the list of winners picked at five tracks across the country using my selection system.

1. **Monmouth:** *Another Boland* paid $5.40 to win in the first race. It was the only horse that had gone today's distance, so it was the sole qualifier according to my system. It had points 1, 2, 4, and 8 in its favor—a standout.

2. **Saratoga:** *Serendip* paid $7.20 to win the second race. It was the sole qualifier because it was the only horse that had gone today's distance. Points 1, 2, 4, 8 and 9 were in its favor, another standout.

3. **Bowie:** *Pet the Jet* won the fifth race, paying $5.40. As it was the only horse that had gone today's distance, it was the sole qualifier. It had points 2, 4, 7, 8 and 10 in its favor, an excellent selection.

4. **Arlington:** *Ax the Fox* paid $12 to win the second race. It was the only one that had gone today's distance, making it the sole qualifier. Having points 2, 4, and 6 in its favor, it was another standout.

5. **Del Mar:** *Ritalistic* and *The Lady Streaker* both qualified at today's distance, so the selection was based on the number of points each had in its favor. *The Lady Streaker* had one point, number 5, in its favor. *Ritalistic* had two points, numbers 2 and 5, on its side. *Ritalistic* was our selection. It paid $8.40 to win the third race.

While this method came up with the morning line favorite in one of the five races, you do not have to "eat chalk" to get a high percentage of winners. Four out of the five horses chosen were not favored. In fact, *Ax the Fox* at Arlington was number nine in the morning line and listed dead last by Sweep in his morning line picks. Yet it was a clear standout according to my system, one that caught the public looking the other way. It paid $12 to win the first race.

The average payoff for the five winners listed above was $7.68 on a $2 ticket; a bettor would have received 5–2 odds on the average payoff. In closing, I am not going to wish you good luck because you already have something better than that—you have a winner for all tracks.

Chapter 10

The Route-Race Burn-Out Theory

By Hal Straus

One of the most subtle, overlooked factors in thoroughbred handicapping is pace. Even the very advanced handicapper will consider past performance elements before attempting to analyze partial times.

Pace is an important basic strategy in race planning, particularly over route distances. Trainers and jockeys commonly discuss pace in pre-race meetings. Factors considered are the desired pace for the horse and the horse's best position in relation to the pace (setting it, pushing it, or remaining well off it until the final turns).

Pace is also used as an offensive weapon. For example, knowing that off-the-pace horses B, C and D cannot mount a successful stretch drive after super-quick fractions gives front runner A a powerful tactical advantage. The advantage may be intensified in the entry situation; one horse can, and often does, set a pace more favorable to another horse in the entry.

Most importantly, the effects of pace operate under physiological laws, particularly over long distances. For example, compared to human long-distance track events, pace has always been basic strategy. From mile races to marathons, runners try to manipulate pace to tire or "burn-out" opponents.

The same holds true in other sports: small, quick, basketball teams continually play fastbreak to wear down bigger, slower teams. Analogies abound in football, tennis, soccer—any sport, such as horse racing, that highlights speed and stamina.

Even with its known strategic implications, pace is given low priority by most horse handicappers. Those oddsmakers would rather analyze class, speed, weight, post position and workouts.

Why do bettors commonly ignore the variable of pace in sport?

(1) Handicappers perceive pace as irrelevant in sprint races. Five- and six-furlong races usually amount to all-out dashes from gate to wire; the jockey has little time to "place" his horse except in vague front or rear positions, which are often dictated by troublesome breaks from the gate. As a result, there is precious little time to recover. Because sprints make up the majority of most racing cards, the bettor does not develop the habit of analyzing pace, nor does he apply it to route races, where pace is very relevant.

This is unfortunate. Even though analyzing partials may not be worth the effort for sprint races, analyzing partials, including sprint partials, can be extremely useful for predicting route results.

(2) Most handicappers, even experienced ones, just don't know how to work with fractions. They are viewed as mathematically complex and time-consuming. Moreover, many long-time handicappers see pace as an uncontrollable and unpredictable variable. They consider it a factor that can change from race to race depending on the front runner's manipulation.

Though these objectives have some validity, learning to deal with partials is not very difficult. Once you have the feel for it, you can determine the pace factor in less than fifteen minutes for most route races.

As for the whimsical nature of pace, the longer route distances yield predictable patterns of pace and position. After all, trainers and jockeys read the *Racing Form* also. The fractions tell them what the pace must be to win. Whim plays a small role in any skilled horseman's decisions—especially for large purses.

(3) Over the years, most handicapper's learn to depend on a standardized system. They evaluate past performance data, compute some sort of uniform rating for each horse, and then predict a winner based on the ratings.

These ratings are much like school exam scores. They are marked on a range from 1–100, without regard to a curve that compares competitors *within the framework* of the present race. Little attempt is made to analyze or foresee the *internal dynamics* of the present race, which should include such factors as probable pace, effects of pace, and off-the-pace positioning.

Analyzing Position Data

The handicapper's first task in analyzing pace for route races is to separate the horses into two groups: (1) front runners, and (2) off-the-pace horses.

This is a relatively simple matter. Most horses develop a pattern for one strategy or another by three years of age. This is quickly revealed by a glance over the *Racing Form* position data.

A typical front runner's position data for his last four races might look like the following:

Horse A

	1/4	1/2	Str.	Fin.
Race 1	1^{hd}	$1^{1/2}$	$2^{1/2}$	$2^{3 1/2}$
Race 2	1^{hd}	$1^{2 1/2}$	1^{5}	1^{7}
Race 3	4^{1}	$3^{1 1/2}$	$2^{1/2}$	2^{3}
Race 4	$2^{1/2}$	$2^{1 1/2}$	$4^{3 1/2}$	4^{6}

In deciding whether a horse should be categorized as a front runner, the bettor should emphasize lengths off-the-lead rather than actual position. For example, in Race 3, Horse A was in fourth position at 1/4-mile, but he was a mere one length off-the-lead. In the other races, Horse A could be classified as a front runner.

A typical off-the-pace horse exhibits position data similar to the following:

Horse B

	1/4	1/2	Str.	Fin.
Race 1	$6^{6 1/2}$	5^{5}	3^{2}	3^{hd}
Race 2	5^{10}	$5^{4 1/4}$	$5^{4 1/4}$	3^{5}
Race 3	$6^{4 1/2}$	4^{2}	$4^{2 1/2}$	$6^{1 3/4}$
Race 4	$11^{8 1/2}$	10^{13}	$8^{7 3/4}$	4^{3}

Of course, in any race, there will be a few horses that show characteristics of both categories and cannot be readily classified:

Horse C

	1/4	1/2	Str.	Fin.
Race 1	$4^{2\frac{1}{2}}$	$4^{1\frac{1}{2}}$	$5^{\frac{3}{4}}$	6^{4}
Race 2	5^{7}	6^{5}	$5^{2\frac{1}{2}}$	$1^{2\frac{1}{4}}$
Race 3	1^{1}	$1^{\frac{1}{2}}$	4^{4}	6^{8}
Race 4	11^{8}	9^{7}	$8^{6\frac{1}{2}}$	$2^{\frac{1}{2}}$

When categorizing grey-area horses, the handicapper notes successes, particularly wins at the same distances as the present race. If the horse had more success running off-the-pace, (as with Horse C in our example), then he should be grouped that way; the horse will generally run off-the-pace in the present race.

Analyzing Fractions

After separating the horses into the two groups, the next step is to find the fastest front runner. This is the horse that will burn-out his rivals during the middle or later stages of the race. Even if the other front runners do not fade badly before the stretch, they will not have, by definition, the necessary late speed or kick to overtake the lead horse.

For example, suppose you are handicapping an eight-horse route over 1-1/8 miles. To determine the front runner's fractions, use the last three races closest in distance to 1-1/8 miles in which the horse was a front runner. (In other words, disregard races in which the horse ran off-the-pace or broke poorly from the gate; these races will not accurately portray front running capabilities.

Use the standard "one length off-the-lead = 1/5 second" formula. With the three sets of fractions, figure an average. Allow for differences in weight carried in the present race (4 pounds = 1/5 second) and track variants.

You will probably arrive at figures similar to the following:

	1/2	3/4
Front runner A	45^4	111
Front runner B	45^1	110^1
Front runner C	46^2	111^1
Front runner D	46	110^4

In this example, front runner B is a clear standout. Any of the other front runners attempting to keep pace with B will drop by the wayside by the 3/4 distance.

Many studies have shown that a front runner with fractional advantages wins almost twice as many races as front runners with slower front-end speed, even with the same final-time rating. Whether this is due to equine physiology, (the effects of attempting to keep a quicker than normal pace on stride, and endurance), or jockey psychology, (the effects of running all-out and still running second or third), can only be conjecture. A combination of these reasons, however, is highly probable.

Your final task is a comparative analysis to determine the effects of early speed on the off-the-pace horses. Specifically, you must decide which of the four off-the-pace horses, if any, have the best chance of closing on the probable 110^1 3/4 fraction. A horse that can only close on a slower time will close on air, not horse flesh.

You can immediately eliminate any off-the-pace horse that has never run a 110^1 six-furlong race. Also overlook horses that never came close to winning a route race with a 110^1 partial by the leader.

Of the remaining horses, the one with the best *final fraction* will be vying with the best front runner at the finish line. You can calculate the final fraction by subtracting 3/4-time from final-time averages over three recent similar distance races.

If no off-the-pace horse can close successfully on a 110^1 partial, the race will most likely be decided by the front runners, wire-to-wire. If the off-the-pace horses can close on partials *better than* 110^1 the early speed will have little effect on the results. Bet on your best off-the-pace horses.

Foreseeing Race Dynamics

By concentrating on pace and position data, you are developing the valuable ability to plot the race before it begins. There are other peripheral factors, of course, that influence internal race dynamics:

(1) *Special jockey abilities.* Certain jockeys are renowned off-the-pace specialists—jockeys who have a sixth sense about when and how to move a horse from far back in the pack. Others are more skilled at setting pace, seeming to own an internal clock that can pare fractions to one-tenth of a second. Recognizing jockey strengths and weaknesses is a valuable pace-handicapping tool and can only be developed through long periods of close observation.

(2) *Track variables.* The length of the stretch run, a measurement sometimes printed in the *Racing Form*, influences dynamics. Specifically, the longer the stretch, the better the chances of the off-the-pace horses. Also, poor track conditions help front running horses, many experts believe, because it is more difficult for off-the-pacers to make up ground already yielded on a sloppy track.

General Pace-Handicapping Tips

(1) The longer the route, the greater the effects of weight, pace, and burn-out. Races 1-1/8 miles and longer are optimum for the theories presented here.

(2) The higher the class of the race and the older the horses, the more effective will be the principles of pace-handicapping.

(3) The bettor should avoid races in which there is no clear fractional advantages—at least 2/5-second.

(4) Sprint partials give the handicapper an extra fraction (the 1/4-mile figure) to take into consideration. This is especially important when deciding between closely-matched front runners.

You will not be able to use pace analysis meaningfully in every race, or even every route race. Perhaps one or two races per week will lend themselves to the burn-out theory. Careful race selection and betting strategy can result in high profits for the informed pace-handicapper.

Horse Racing Terminology

ALTERED TICKETS—Invalid pari-mutuel tickets with information changed in an attempt to match valid tickets for cashing.

AUCTION POOLS (calcuttas)—System used in lieu of pari-mutuel system to wager.

BACKSTRETCH—The straightaway farthest from the finish line. Often used to describe the barn area.

BANKROLL—A set sum of money used to carry on business daily at racetracks. Also used to describe money available to an individual for the sole purpose of gambling.

BERTILLION CARD—A card kept on record with identifying marks, scars, etc., used in making positive identification of an animal.

BREAK—Term used for the beginning of a race.

BREAKAGE—Monies in excess of actual payoffs for winning tickets. Prices calculated to nearest dime or nickel according to laws governing particular tracks.

BREAKER—A horse who consistently leaves the starting box or gate rapidly at the start of a race.

BREEDERS—Persons engaged in breeding and raising racing animals.

BREEDERS AWARDS—Monies set aside from purses paid winning horses, and paid to original breeder of winning animal.

BUG—Name denoting the reduced weight allowance permitted an apprentice jockey.

BUSH TRACKS—Tracks holding horse races where the pari-mutuel system of wagering is not authorized. Any form of gambling on these races is illegal.

CASH-SELL—Name used to describe system whereby a customer is able to purchase pari-mutuel tickets and cash valid tickets at the same window.

CATCH DRIVERS—A free lance driver who is available to drive for other owners and trainers. Race driving is his primary occupation.

CLAIMING RACE—Races where horses are entered with the agreement to actually sell the horse to any other bona fide owner or trainer for the price stipulated in the conditions of the race. Claims must be made in accordance with the rules of racing at the track where the claim is made.

CLASSIFIED RACING—New concept of assigning grades to standardbred horses to make up races so that horses are equally matched.

CLUBHOUSE TURN—The turn entering the backstretch from the front stretch.

COLORS—Color combinations of shirts and caps worn by the jockey in thoroughbred races. These colors represent a particular owner for all horses running in his name and are registered with the Jockey Club.

COLTS—An unaltered male horse under 4 years of age.

COMMERCIAL TRACKS—Term used to designate a track using the pari-mutuel system to provide monies necessary to carry on a racing meet.

COMMISSION—Monies deducted from pari-mutuel pools to pay expenses and revenue necessary to conduct a racing meet.

CONDITION BOOK—A book containing specific conditions that must be met in order to enter a horse in future races scheduled to be run on a specified date.

CONSOLATION POOLS—Applies to pools involving two or more races. Holders of tickets having the correct selections in the races completed, but whose selection is a late scratch in the later race or races, share in a portion of the profits of that particular pool.

COOL OUT—Methods used after a race, primarily bathing and walking, to gradually cool out a horse. Prevents stiffness and soreness of animals after competition.

DASH HEAT—A tie by two or more entries in a race.

DASH RACE—A standardbred race where the order of finish is determined by one heat only.

DROPS—Racetrack term used to describe errors in money transactions between customers and clerks, and where these errors are in favor of the clerks.

EXOTIC POOLS—Mutuel pools other than the conventional win, place, and show pools. Involves more than one entry—examples: daily double, exactas, trifectas.

FAVORITE—Entry having more dollars bet on it than any other entry in the race.

FILLY—A female horse under 4 years of age.

FILM PATROL—Pictures taken from various angles during the running of a race to help stewards determine infractions of the rules.

FINAL LINE—Win odds when betting has been completed for any particular race.

FINISHER (CLOSER)—Term used to describe horses who usually give their best effort during the later stages of a race.

FIRST TURN—The turn first entered after a race has started. Location varies due to the length of the race and size of the track.

FOUL CLAIM—A claim by a jockey, owner or trainer that their order of finish in a race was adversely affected by a rules infraction by another rider or driver in the same race. This claim is considered by the stewards and a decision rendered before a race is declared official.

FRACTIONS—Time consumed in running different portions of a race.

FRESH—An entry who has not raced in some time.

FRESH MONEY—Money brought to the track for wagering by the customers. Excludes money bet by customers from winnings earlier in the racing program.

FRIVOLOUS FOUL CLAIM—A claim of foul with absolutely no justification. Often results in a fine for the party lodging the complaint.

GAIT—A way of stepping in a given manner. Applies to race horses as to whether trotting, pacing, or running.

GAMBLER—One who wagers on the outcome of a race, game or contest of any kind.

GELDING—A castrated male horse.

HANDICAPPER—A person who projects his selections in races or games based on information of past performances of entries.

HANDICAPS—Thoroughbred races where weight carried by each horse is assigned by the racing secretary to give each entry as equal a chance as possible.

HANDLE—Term used by race tracks to designate volume of monies wagered. Applies to race, day or season totals.

HAND TICKETS—Pre-printed pari-mutuel tickets used before automated equipment was available to print tickets at the time they were purchased.

HORSE—An unaltered male horse 4 years old or older.

HORSEMAN'S BOOKKEEPER—A person who keeps an up-to-date record of each owner's money during a racing meet. Credits amount earned in purses, debits deductions for jock mounts, claims, etc.

JOCKEY—One who is licensed to ride a thoroughbred or quarter horse during an official race.

JOCK MOUNTS—Standard fees for a jockey to ride a thoroughbred or quarter horse during an official race.

LAY OFF MONEY—Money bet by a bookmaker at a track or with another bookmaker when he has accepted more bets on one particular entry than he feels is safe for his operation.

LONG SHOT—Entry not well-regarded by the bettors in a race or game, resulting in high odds and large payoffs should he finish 1st, 2nd, or 3rd.

MARES—Female horse 4 years old or older.

MARGINAL TRACKS—A track whose volume of business is low enough that profits and continued operation are questionable.

MATCH RACE—A race between two horses. Held at tracks other than commercial ones, with rare exceptions. Such races are not subject to rules of racing in their particular state, when pari-mutuel betting is not used for this type of race.

MATINEES—Afternoon racing at tracks where night racing is the usual practice.

MINUS POOLS—When there are not enough profits left in a pool to pay the minimum price to holders of winning tickets, as required by law. Losses are actually made up from breakage from other pools.

MOONLIGHTERS—Track employees having steady employment in other fields and using track and fronton earnings as a supplement to their regular income.

MORNING LINE—Odds quoted prior to any actual betting by customers. A handicapper's assessment of approximately what odds an entry will be at post time, based on the bets made by the public.

MULTIPLE BETTING—The practice of a bettor backing several combinations in the same race. Pertains chiefly to exotic pools.

MUTILATED TICKETS—Pari-mutuel tickets partially destroyed, usually torn, to the extent that necessary information on the ticket for cashing is not complete.

ODDS—Number indicating amount of profit per dollar to be paid to holders of winning pari-mutuel tickets.

ODDS BOARD (PUBLIC DISPLAY BOARD)—Facilities in the infield of a track or at other locations visible to the public, to post information regarding odds, pay-offs, sometimes advertising, or any other information pertinent to the operation of tracks.

OFF-TRACK—Term used for two different situations. Either when a track's surface is at less than its best potential due to rain or other weather factors or to denote business being conducted in direct relation to the track's business at a location other than the track itself.

OFF-TRACK BETTING (OTB)—Legal wagering at a location other than the track where the races are being held. Must conform to the rules and regulations of the states involved.

OUTRIDERS—Employees of track who assist and supervise jockeys and horses during post parade from the paddock to the starting gate. Responsible for catching runaways and horses who have lost their riders.

OUT TICKETS—Winning pari-mutuel tickets not presented to cashiers for payment before the close of current day's business.

OVERLAY—An entry whose odds are higher than those estimated by professional handicappers.

OVERPAY—A case where the price paid to winning ticket holders is more than the correct price, due to computer or human error.

OVERWEIGHTS—Term used in horse racing where jockeys are involved. The term is used when a horse will carry more weight than the minimum authorized by the set conditions of a race; dictated by the fact that the jockey being used cannot reduce his weight enough to ride at the assigned weight.

PADDOCK—Area of assembly for horses immediately before a race. Thoroughbreds and quarter horses are saddled and turned over to the jockeys. Final instructions are given to riders and drivers. Entries receive a final identification check in this area.

PARI-MUTUEL—A system of betting, whereby the holders of winning tickets are paid in proportion to the sums they have wagered.

PAST PERFORMANCE—Documented records of previous efforts of horses.

PER CAPITA—Average amount bet by each customer during a day's business at a racetrack.

PHOTO FINISH—System of taking pictures of the finish of a race too close to determine the winners by the naked eye.

PIGEON—An invalid ticket paid by mistake to a customer by a cashier.

PLACING JUDGE—A racing official responsible for determining the correct order of finish of a race.

PLATER—Name often used for a blacksmith.

POST PARADE—Used to describe the field of horses going from the paddock to the starting gate or starting box.

POST TIME—Time designated to start the first race or game of the day and all races or games subsequently during that day's business.

PURSE—Prize money earned by winning horses.

RACETRACKER—A name often used for one whose interests and income are almost totally connected with racing in one department or another.

RACING COMMISSION—An appointed body of men and women which governs and polices racing and jai alai in states where legislation has been passed to permit use of the parimutuel system in connection with these sports. Usually appointed by the governor of the state.

RACING DATES—Specific dates allotted to horse and dog tracks to conduct business by Racing Commissions charged with granting licenses and monitoring the conduct of these tracks in conformation with the official rules of racing in their states.

RAIL RUNNER—A horse with a history of running near the inside rail of a track whenever conditions permit.

REPLAYS—Films of races played back for the benefit of fans and officials after the completion of a race.

RULES OF RACING—Official rules approved by the body responsible for the conduct of racing in conformance with the legislation permitting these races to be held—in most cases, a Racing Commission.

SCHOOLING RACES—Practice races held using actual racing conditions, but in which no wagering is allowed.

SCRATCH—An entry listed to compete in a race, but withdrawn after becoming an official entry, due to illness, injury, or other bona fide reasons.

SPRINTER (EARLY SPEED)—Term used to describe horses who usually give their best effort during the early stages of a race.

STEWARDS—Racing officials charged with the duty of making sure races are carried out in conformance with rules set down by the Racing Commission in the state where these contests are being held.

STEWARD'S INQUIRY—Situation where stewards suspect infractions of rules during a horse race. Race is not declared official until stewards have studied the film made of the race and have questioned the jockeys or drivers involved. If suspicions are confirmed, violators are disqualified, and a new order of finish is posted.

STOOPERS—Name given to persons looking for valid tickets discarded mistakenly by patrons at a track or fronton. This practice is prohibited by law in most states.

STRAGGLERS—Valid tickets not cashed before the next contest is held, but cashed before the day's business is completed.

STRETCH—The straightaway portion of a racetrack from the final turn to the finish line.

TACK—Equipment used in the training and racing of horses; jockeys refer to their helmets, boots, whips, etc., as their "tack."

TACK ROOMS—Name given to rooms in the barn area of a racetrack in which items necessary for the training and racing of horses are kept.

TEN PERCENTERS—Name given to those signing IRS forms for actual owners of tickets paying off at odds of 300–1 or more, for a share of the pay-off, usually 10%. Practice prohibited by law.

THOROUGHBREDS—A breed of horses registered by recognized Jockey Clubs. Used for racing at a running gait.

TIP SHEETS—Selections of professional handicappers for sale to patrons desiring help in deciding which entry to wager on.

TOUTS—Persons furnishing their selections to patrons in return for a portion of the amount of money collected, should their selections win. Practice discouraged at all tracks and illegal at most.

TRACK CONDITION—Refers to condition of a track used for racing horses. Conditions vary due to rain or other climatic factors. Examples: fast, sloppy, muddy, heavy, etc.

TRAINERS—Persons in charge of conditioning horses and dogs in preparation for official races.

TRIPLE CROWN—Term used to describe the three most prestigious stake races for three-year-old thoroughbreds in the U.S.

Namely, the "Kentucky Derby," the "Preakness" and the "Belmont Stakes."

UNDERLAY—A horse whose odds are lower than those estimated by professional handicappers.

UNDERPAY—A case where the price paid winning ticket holders is less than the correct price, due to computer or human error.

UPPER TURN—Designates turn entering the stretch leading to the finish line.

WEIGH IN—Term used for checking a jockey's weight before and after a race.

Part Three
SPORTS WAGERING

WHAT YOU WILL FIND IN THIS SECTION

In the following pages, two noted handicapping experts reveal their winning handicapping techniques for baseball and jai alai.

Part Three
SPORTS WAGERING

JAI ALAI

Jai alai is a tempestuous sport that requires courage, stamina, agility, cunning and untiring endurance. A good player needs split-second timing and coordination. It is the world's fastest game. A player on the court is in constant motion. In the American game, played for seven points, a player will run a mile a game, usually playing four games a night on the typical fronton card. On matinee days he doubles his mileage. This physical effort should be contrasted with that of a race horse running six furlongs once a week, or a lazy right fielder in baseball who might shag a couple of flies in an entire game. There is no comparison with the strenuous demands of jai alai. Even football players, with their offensive and defensive switching of teams and playing one game a week, have it easy compared with the pelotari who is on the card six days a week. No other game requires as much energy or endurance.

Chapter 11

Plush Perfecta

By Bill Keevers

Wasn't it Duffy's Tavern where they had the sign that said: "Where the elite meet to eat." Visit any fronton and you'll find an exclusive place where the phi beta kappas of the jai alai fraternity gather to place their scholarly bets at the separated windows.

In jai alai, the most popular betting pastime is the quiniela (Q), with its 28 possible winning combinations. In that system, where you pick two equally important numbers, the 28 possibles boil down to naked odds of 27 to 1. With the Q, it doesn't matter which of your selections finishes first. With the trifecta, that exact three-number formula, there are 336 possible winners, so it's a real long shot if a single number comes through. Boxing the trifecta numbers reduces the odds and the payoff.

In the perfecta, a betting system that is something special, there are 56 possible winning combinations. The raw odds are 55 to 1; you pick two numbers, but they must finish in the exact order in which you choose them. If you pick 3 and 2, the #3 team must definitely come in first and the second finisher must be #2. If #2 wins and #3 comes in afterward, that's too bad and you lose.

If you had been smart enough to reverse your bet—play it both ways, which most of the perfecta players actually do—then you would have won. With a reversed combination in the perfecta, the adjusted odds are 28 to 1. It would cost you $3 to play a one-way perfecta; $6 if you were to reverse the play.

Perfecta players at jai alai are the professional handicappers. They figure everything out precisely and leave very little to chance. They are the aristocrats of the jai alai bettors, the precisionists, the human computers. Seasoned perfecta players never pick their numbers out of a hat or play seat numbers. They come to a betting conclusion only after a great deal of sound reasoning as to why they should play the 6 and 2 or the 5 and 4 in a particular game. It is never a random choice.

These perfectionists are intelligent people. They project winning combinations by logic, deduction, inference and analysis. Perfecta players have formidable reasoning powers. Because the system caters to these intellects, you will find 100 or more betting windows that will take your wagers on a quiniela, win, place or show, or trifecta.

For the elite perfecta player, you'll probably find a single window at one end of the betting level, and possibly one more window at the other end. There aren't that many shrewd mathematicians walking around, so two windows on each floor will take care of them. They are the Ph.D.'s of jai alai—they play it precisely high and deep.

What's a perfecta? It's that tantalizing betting system where you pick two numbers (two teams) and match your dollars with your wits. As mentioned, it is clever to play the reverse combination just in case. With reverse play, you win one, lose one, but the payoff usually supports the risk. Don't be surprised about the other names; in some states, if this betting system is called the exacta, or correcta, it is because the word "perfecta" might be registered there for something else (like a cigar or some other existing legal priority).

The perfecta system of betting is an old Spanish custom. Like its cousin, the quiniela, it originated in the U.S. at the jai alai games in Florida during the 1930s. The brother in the horse racing and greyhound gentry quickly adopted this interesting form of betting as a wagering innovation. For a long time, the average return on a winning perfecta ticket was $115 for a $3 bet. Today, it seems to be getting higher as the perfecta is a little harder to figure out.

On a recent night at Dania, that elegantly modernized fronton in Florida, six of the twelve games on the card produced a perfecta payoff of over $200. Unusual, but there it was. At the same fronton, when newspaper results showed a 7-6 perfecta payoff of $750.50, a skeptical fan called the office to verify the price thinking it was a misprint. An officer quickly assured him the price was right. "Is that a record?" the astonished caller asked. "Oh, no," came the answer, "we've had perfectas that paid over $1,000."

Not very often, mind you, but a high payoff has happened. With a friendly computer, playing long shot numbers like 7-8 or 6-7 might net you a bundle. Of course, to be cautious, there have been $40 perfecta payoffs, too—just a situation where too many people had the same numbers and the pool had to be subdivided among a lot of single-minded players.

No matter which betting system you follow in jai alai, certain number combinations are going to come out more often than others. Low numbers win more often than high numbers on the average for a simple reason: Low-numbered teams come back on the floor in the round robin eliminations more often than the higher-numbered teams. Veteran jai alai fans do not overlook the relative individual merits of the players involved, and this remains a handicapping factor.

Do certain numbers come out winners at different frontons more often than others? The answer is yes. Study the statistics in the program wherever you're at for the local pattern. Most gamblers favor the theory that lucky numbers repeat. While favored numbers may vary fronton to fronton, it *is* surprising how often the same combinations come up even in different places. Mathematicians are quick to spot the predominance of the lower numbers such as 3 and 2.

It is smart to note that for some reason the higher number in a perfecta combination comes out first more often than the lower number. The ratio could be 2 to 1, sometimes even higher. The appended comparative figures for perfecta results at two different frontons, Milford and Hartford, both in Connecticut, were 3-2 at both frontons. We found that this leading perfecta combination came through over the entire season. (See Figure 11-1.)

The 4-3 combo was tied for first at Milford and a strong second at Hartford. For third place it was 3-1 at Hartford, 4-1 at Milford. In fourth place, it was the 2-1 combination at each fronton—more than a coincidence. The fifth-place winner at Hartford was 5-1; its counterpart in fifth place was 5-2 at Milford. That's pretty close.

These figures carry a message. No number over 5 was in these top brackets. That doesn't mean that the 6-7-8 numbers don't come in. They do come in, and they pay big when they hit. The lower numbers, however, win more often. These are the teams that come back on the

Figure 11-1

Comparative Results of Perfecta (Exacta) Wins

Full season — 1979
First 15 combinations

HARTFORD FRONTON			MILFORD FRONTON		
Sequence	Winning Number	Number of Wins	Sequence	Winning Number	Number of Wins
1.	3 - 2	88	1.	3 - 2	88
2.	4 - 2	83	2.	4 - 2	88
3.	3 - 1	73	3.	4 - 1	87
4.	2 - 1	72	4.	2 - 1	84
5.	5 - 1	70	5.	5 - 2	77
6.	1 - 2	68	6.	5 - 3	77
7.	2 - 3	65	7.	6 - 3	77
8.	1 - 3	64	8.	6 - 2	76
9.	4 - 1	64	9.	5 - 1	71
10.	5 - 3	63	10.	3 - 1	70
11.	5 - 2	61	11.	1 - 2	68
12.	1 - 5	60	12.	8 - 5	68
13.	6 - 2	59	13.	7 - 4	65
14.	7 - 4	59	14.	2 - 7	64
15.	6 - 3	58	15.	6 - 4	64

High numbers on top 11 times (out of 15).

High numbers on top 13 times (out of 15).

floor more often—the old percentage factor. The payoffs will vary. Play the favorite numbers, and the price will be lower. Play the long shot, and the payoff should be fatter.

There may be a scientific reason why the higher number in a perfecta combination comes in first more often than the lower number, but nobody seems to know the answer. The compilation covering an entire season shows the direct comparison—the exact record between the performance of the high number in any combination versus the low number.

In the 28 two-digit combinations, the high number came in first 24 times, the low number only 4. The only exceptions were the 1-7 combination which won 41 times, versus the 7-1 which won only 36 times; another was the 2-7 which won 64 times, against 7-2 which won 42 times; the third was 3-8 which won 41 times, over 8-3 which won 30 times; the fourth and last was 6-7, another 7 which came in first 18 times compared with its alternate 7-6 which occurred 16 times. Mathematicians might make a note of the sevens in this sample—three out of four.

Look at Figure 11-2. The 7-8 combination won only 11 times. Other small winners were the 5-8, 15 times; and 6-8, also 15 times. By contrast, note that 3-2 and 4-2 won 88 times. This was 11 times more than the 7-8. (Payoffs, of course, reflected these variations.)

It seems the high number will win over 60% of the time. The 8-5 combination won 68 times; its reverse combo, 5-8, won only 15 times—an 82% margin.

Let's look at 5-3 with 77 winners against the 3-5 which came in only 26 times—a 74% advantage. Its neighbor, 6-3, won 77 times; its reverse, 3-6, won only 24 times—a 77% winning percentage. The combo that won more than any other, the 1-2 and 2-1 twosome, racked up a total of 152 wins. Two-1 won 84 times; 1-2 won 68 times, but here the high-number advantage was only 55%.

Other "lucky" combinations, 2-4 and 4-2, had 139 wins combined. The 2-3, 3-2 double had 138 wins. Next to those, the 2-5 and 5-2 had 129 wins. One-4 and 4-1 gathered in 126 wins; that's the same number as the 2-6 and 6-2 combo. One-5 and 5-1 totalled 123 payoffs; the 1-3 and 3-1 duo had 119 wins. On the low side, 7-8 and 8-7 could account for only 31 wins; the 6-7 and 7-6 combination made it only 34 times.

A clever bettor at a fronton, where the "high-number-first" result prevails, plays the perfecta this way: He buys two tickets on the high-number combination and a single ticket on the low-high number. If his numbers come in, he's got a winner either way. If the high-number-first combination wins, and it does on the average, then he has a double profit.

Figure 11-2

Perfecta Results at an Eastern Fronton				
Low Number First	Wins	High Number First	Wins	Total for Both
1 - 2	68	2 - 1	84	152
1 - 3	49	3 - 1	70	119
1 - 4	39	4 - 1	87	126
1 - 5	52	5 - 1	71	123
1 - 6	46	6 - 1	63	109
1 - 7*	41	7 - 1	36	77
1 - 8	48	8 - 1	53	101
2 - 3	50	3 - 2	88	138
2 - 4	51	4 - 2	88	139
2 - 5	52	5 - 2	77	129
2 - 6	50	6 - 2	76	126
2 - 7*	64	7 - 2	42	106
2 - 8	50	8 - 2	53	103
3 - 4	40	4 - 3	45	85
3 - 5	26	5 - 3	77	103
3 - 6	24	6 - 3	77	101
3 - 7	36	7 - 3	58	94
3 - 8*	41	8 - 3	30	71
4 - 5	18	5 - 4	49	67
4 - 6	18	6 - 4	64	82
4 - 7	29	7 - 4	55	84
4 - 8	27	8 - 4	54	81
5 - 6	17	6 - 5	35	52
5 - 7	23	7 - 5	44	67
5 - 8	15	8 - 5	68	83
6 - 7*	18	7 - 6	16	34
6 - 8	15	8 - 6	49	64
7 - 8	11	8 - 7	20	31

*In 28 combinations, the low number in first position won more games only four times.

There you have it—the jai alai perfecta; it's a gambling adventure that can return your invested capital many times. Any wager that can double your money is attractive, but in the perfecta you're shooting for a prize that will bring back 30 or 40 times the amount you are risking, and maybe a lot more.

It takes a little figuring, but the incentive is there. When you turn in a ticket that costs you $3 and watch the cashier pile up the twenties, while he's counting $120, $180, $210, it's a grand and glorious feeling.

When you come to jai alai, don't overlook the perfecta. It gives you more for your money.

Jai Alai Terminology

BANKROLL—A set sum of money used to carry on business daily at frontons. Also used to describe money available to an individual for the sole purpose of gambling.

BREAKAGE—Monies in excess of actual payoffs for winning tickets. Prices calculated to nearest dime or nickel according to laws governing particular frontons.

CANCHA—Playing area of a jai alai fronton.

CESTA—A combination glove and basket type object, strapped to the wrist of a jai alai player, used to catch and throw the ball *(pelota)* during a jai alai contest.

COMMISSION—Monies deducted from pari-mutuel pools to pay expenses and revenue necessary to conduct a jai alai operation.

FAVORITE—Entry having more dollars bet on it than any other entry in the game.

FRONTIS—Front wall of a cancha at jai alai frontons.

FRONTON—Name of building where jai alai is played.

HANDLE—Term used by frontons to designate volume of monies wagered.

JAI ALAI—A game of Basque origin used in some countries for pari-mutuel wagering in the same manner as horse or dog racing.

LATERAL—Name used for the side wall of the cancha at a jai alai fronton.

MOONLIGHTERS—Fronton employees having steady employment in other fields and using fronton earnings as a supplement to their regular income.

ODDS—Number indicating amount of profit per dollar to be paid to holders of winning pari-mutuel tickets.

PARI-MUTUEL—A system of betting, whereby the holders of winning tickets are paid in proportion to the sums they have wagered.

PARTIDO SYSTEM—Jai alai games played by two individuals or two sets of partners only. The winner is decided when one player or one team has reached a pre-designated number of points (usually 25 to 35 points). It is not possible to use the pari-mutuel system for partido games except for win pools.

PAST PERFORMANCE—Documented records of previous efforts of jai alai players.

PELOTA—Ball used to play jai alai.

PER CAPITA—Average amount bet by each customer during a day's business at a fronton.

PURSE—Prize money earned by winning jai alai players.

RACING COMMISSION—An appointed body of men and women which governs and polices jai alai in states where legislation has been passed to permit use of the pari-mutuel system in connection with this sport. Usually appointed by the governor of the state.

REBOTE—Back wall of a cancha at a jai alai fronton.

SCRATCH—An entry listed to compete in a game, but withdrawn after becoming an official entry, due to illness, injury, or other bona fide reasons.

STEWARDS—Racing officials charged with the duty of making sure jai alai games are carried out in conformance with rules set down by the Racing Commission in the state where these contests are being held.

STOOPERS—Name given to persons looking for valid tickets discarded mistakenly by patrons at a fronton. This practice is prohibited by law in most states.

TIP SHEETS—Selections of professional handicappers for sale to patrons desiring help in deciding which entry to wager on.

TOUTS—Persons furnishing their selections to patrons in return for a portion of the amount of money collected, should their selections win. Practice discouraged at all frontons and illegal at most.

BASEBALL

Baseball is by far the easiest sport to win at for several reasons. The main one is that all you must do to be a winner is select the team that does in fact win the game. That may sound ridiculously obvious to some of you; but remember that when one is wagering on a football or a basketball game, one must beat the pointspread to win. In baseball, this is not the case; one simply lays or takes odds on the teams he expects to win the game.

Another factor that sets major league baseball apart from other sports is the long, 162-game schedule. Baseball teams play six days a week for six straight months. Football teams, on the other hand, play a mere fourteen games during the regular season. With so many more games in baseball, the handicapper has a much larger sampling to analyze and from which to draw conclusions, and he can spot trends more easily than he might in other sports.

Chapter 12

Pitching Situations to Look For

By Ernie Kaufman

When it comes to selecting a team, many baseball handicappers will tell you that the most important factor to consider is the two starting pitchers in the game in question. They can and will refer to a myriad of commonly known statistics such as the pitcher's earned run average; won-lost records against each individual team; how each pitcher fared in day games as compared to night games; or astro-turf versus natural grass.

The list goes on and on with many other interesting statistics. But there's a problem. Although these stats appear to give a bettor an edge in daily handicapping, all this information can be confusing.

Readily available statistics on recent pitching results may offer a slight edge in handicapping. They do not, however, avail the sports gamer with any definite advantage. There are two very apparent reasons for this:

(1) The people who create the lines in Nevada, and probably your local bookmaker, too, are already aware of these same statistics. Thus, they will adjust the odds on the games accordingly. For example, if Steve Carlton totally dominates the St. Louis Cardinals, then you will pay a very heavy price in the odds if you wanted to bet Carlton against the Cardinals.

(2) The general public is also aware of these trends because of increased awareness to such statistics. Once again, let's use the Carlton example.

The gaming public will heavily back Carlton when he goes against the Cardinals, causing an already over-stated line to move even more drastically than it should. This is why we see so many baseball games where the betting lines are 2 to 1 or more, or even from 1 to 2-1/2 runs.

I have always believed that run lines in baseball were extremely overstated; and thus, that they were a sucker play if you were looking to bet the favorite. It is just too much to give any major league team a 1 or 2 spot in a game.

If you were to take the runs (underdogs) in all of the run line games during the two seasons studied (1979-1980), you would have won 56% of your plays. That's nothing to retire on. It is, however, substantially profitable with very little handicapping effort.

If all the publicly known statistics are not the answer to good handicapping, then what can the baseball bettor rely on for winning information?

One way to successfully select winning baseball teams is to look for key elements. These elements should directly affect either a starting pitcher or the team that he is going against. There are many such situations available to the baseball handicapper; following are two of the very best.

The After Knuckleball Theory

Several seasons ago, Pete Rose was involved in a 44-game hitting streak. He said he was most worried about the game he would play after he had faced a knuckleball pitcher. Rose said that facing a knuckleball pitcher ruined a hitter's timing: "It's the next game in which you pay the penalty, because your timing is off."

Such an obvious physical factor, coming from possibly the best hitter in baseball, gives the sports handicapper an equally obvious great betting situation. The strategy here is to bet against any team who plays a game immediately after playing any pitcher who is a knuckleball-type thrower.

What we are doing here is betting against an entire team that is having a problem with their timing. Such plays have rendered a strong 64% in winning bets over the three seasons of 1978, 1979 and 1980. The beauty of this winning percentage is that, in most cases, you were playing an underdog because the knuckleball pitchers' teams usually do not command a strong betting line.

The Big Contract Theory

Let us suppose that John Doe works as a salesman for Company A. John feels that he could be earning a larger salary from any of Company A's competitors. The question is: Should John go to the president of Company A in an attempt to negotiate a raise? Or should he go to Company A's competitors, namely Companies B, C, D and E, and offer his services for more money than he now earns?

Most likely, John would ask his own company for the raise, because the other companies would probably not appreciate John's offer. They may feel that John will dump them, too, for another company in the future.

Such is not the case in major league baseball. Because of the "free agent" clause, a player can actually play out his contract with his current team, put his services up for grabs to the highest bidder among all the baseball teams, and then go to whichever team he so desires.

Obviously, such an involved negotiation procedure has some psychological effects on the players that are involved in this free agent status. During the last year of their present contracts, players attempt to inflate their cash value to all the teams that are interested in them. The free agents will be working extra hard for good statistics during the season.

Some baseball players who had phenomenal seasons during their option years were Don Sutton, Nolan Ryan, Tommy John, Bert Blyleven, Don Stanhouse and Dave Goltz. Notice how some of them never regained their option season successes once they got their big contracts signed. What's happening here is obvious: a form of complacency sets in once the players get the "big bucks" guaranteed to them.

This is a form of normal human behavior. A person works hard at something until they are successful at it. Once that goal is attained, they either relax or look elsewhere to put their energies.

As sports bettors, we want to bet any starting pitcher who is playing out his option year, which is the final year of his contract with his current team. We also want to bet against any starting pitcher during his first year of a big contract with any team—even his own.

There you have two proven theories, one physical, the other psychological in nature. They have generated profits for the baseball wagerer in the past. Apply them to your current handicapping system and they may make your baseball season a more enjoyable experience.

Baseball Terminology

ADVANCE—The moving ahead of a base runner to the next base as a result of a hit, error, sacrifice, balk, etc.

AHEAD—To be winning; a pitcher can be ahead in the count if he has more strikes on the batter than balls.

ALLEY—The space between the center fielder and right fielder or between the center fielder and left fielder.

AROUND THE HORN—A phrase describing a ball thrown from third base to second base to first base, generally in a double-play situation.

ASSIST—A player's throw to another player on his team that results in a putout.

AT BAT—An official time up at the plate as a hitter.

AWAY—A pitch out of the reach of a batter. A side retired in its half of an inning.

BACKSTOP—Another name for the position of catcher.

BALK—Illegal movement by a pitcher that, when executed with runner(s) on base, allows the runner(s) to advance one base with the bases empty; a ball is added to the count of the batter.

BASE—The white canvas bags, set 90 feet apart in professional baseball, and designated as 1st base, 2nd base, and 3rd base.

BASE HIT—Any fair hit that results in a player reaching a base safely; generally refers to a single (BINGLE).

BASE ON BALLS—The yielding of a fourth pitch outside the strike zone to a batter, which allows him to move to first base.

BASES LOADED—A situation where there are runners on 1st, 2nd, and 3rd base.

BASKET CATCH—A catch of a ball by an outfielder with glove at waist level, palm side up; made famous by Willie Mays.

BAT AROUND—A situation where each batter in the lineup receives a chance to hit in the same inning.

BAT BOY/GIRL—A youngster who takes care of bats and other baseball equipment.

BATTER—The player who is up at bat, hitting (BATSMAN).

BATTER'S BOX—A rectangle on either side of home plate in which the batter must stand in order to hit.

BATTERY—The pitcher and catcher.

BATTERY MATE—The catcher is the pitcher's battery mate; the pitcher is the catcher's battery mate.

BATTING AVERAGE—A means of indicating the effectiveness of a hitter. To compute the average, the number of hits is divided by the number of official times at bat.

BATTING ORDER—The sequence in which hitters on a team come to bat in a game.

BEAN—To strike a batter in the head with a pitched ball.

BEANBALL—A pitched ball aimed generally at the head of a batter.

BELT—The hitting of a ball with much force by a batter.

BLANK—To shut out; to hold the opposition scoreless (WHITEWASH).

BLAST—A very powerfully hit ball that travels for distance.

BLOCK THE PLATE—The act of a catcher straddling the baseline between home plate and an oncoming base runner in an attempt to be in a good position to tag out the runner.

BLOOPER—A softly hit ball that generally has some backspin and which barely drops in beyond the infield. A lobbed pitch.

BOTTOM—The second half of an inning; the time reserved for the home team to bat.

BREAKING PITCH—A pitch that does not come in straight to a batter, but moves about, such as a curve or a slider.

BRUSHBACK PITCH—As opposed to a beanball, a pitch not thrown *at* the batter, but thrown close enough to him to make him move back from a too choice position in the batter's box.

BULLET—A hard-thrown fastball. A powerfully hit ball.

BULLPEN—An area, generally in the left or right field vicinity, where relief pitchers are allowed to warm up during a game in case they are needed to come in and pitch.

BUNT—To tap, but not swing, at a ball to get it to roll just a bit onto the playing field. Bunters can try to make it to first safely, in order to get a bunt hit, or they may place the ball in such a way as to sacrifice or give themselves up while moving a teammate up to another base.

BUSH LEAGUES—The low minor leagues or not well-known leagues.

CALL—Announcement of an umpire, or the keeping track of balls and strikes.

CALLED STRIKE—A pitch that a batter does not swing at but which is announced as a strike by the umpire.

CATCHER—The player positioned behind home plate who catches the ball thrown by the pitcher.

CHANCE—A fielder's opportunity to catch a ball.

CHEST PROTECTOR—A stuffed pad worn over the chest by catchers and umpires to ward off damage from thrown or batted balls.

CHOKE UP—To grip the bat nearer to the middle than down at the handle in order to get better bat control. To panic in stress situations.

CHOP—To smash the ball down onto the ground.

CLEAN-UP HITTER—The fourth man in the batting order.

COACH'S BOXES—Rectangular boxes eight feet outside first base and third base in which the coaches of the team at bat stand, giving signals and advice to the batters and base runners.

COMPLETE GAME—A game that a pitcher starts and finishes.

CORNER—The inside and the outside portions of home plate.

COUNT—The number of balls and strikes on a batter during his turn at bat.

CROWDING THE PLATE—A situation where a player moves up close to the plate, either to increase his chances of walking or his ability to hit an outside pitch.

CURVEBALL—A pitch that breaks and curves as it crosses the plate.

CUT—A batter's swing.

CUT DOWN—A fielder's throw that results in a base runner being put out in the act of trying to reach the next base.

CUT OFF—A throw, usually from an outfielder to a catcher, that is stopped by an infielder on its way to the catcher or infielder.

CYCLE—A batter achieving a single, double, triple, and home run in the same game.

DEAD BALL—A ball that does not carry far. A ball that is out of play either because play has been temporarily suspended or because the ball is outside the boundaries of play.

DELAYED STEAL—A stolen base executed after the pitcher has thrown the ball to the catcher and not while the pitch is underway, as in a traditional stolen base.

DESIGNATED HITTER—A rule in the American League that allows a team to designate a batter to hit for the pitcher, the designated hitter doesn't play in the field and the pitcher never comes to bat.

DIAMOND—The baseball infield, whose four bases resemble the points of a diamond in the shape they outline.

DIE—A situation where a runner is left on base at the end of an inning because his batting teammates cannot score him. A situation where a baseball drops abruptly in its flight.

DIG IN—The act of a batter getting firmer footing in the batter's box by using the spikes on his shoes to loosen the ground. Metaphorically, a situation where a batter bears down in his concentration against a pitcher.

DOUBLE—A hit that allows a player to run from the batter's box to second base.

DOUBLEHEADER—Two games played on the same day, usually right after each other and usually for a single admission price for the fan.

DOUBLE PLAY—The retiring of two players for two outs on the same play.

DOUBLE STEAL—A situation where two base runners each steal a base on the same play.

DOWN—Losing or out ("one man down in the top of the ninth"), or trailing in the score ("down by three runs").

DRAG BUNT—A ball purposely hit slowly by a batter facing away from the pitcher to give himself a head start in his run to first base in pursuit of a hit.

DRIVE—A batted ball hit for distance.

DRIVE IN—To bat a run in, to cause a run to score.

DUGOUT—An area on each side of home plate where players stay while their team is at bat. There is a visitors' dugout and a home-team dugout.

DUSTER—A pitch thrown high and inside to a batter and intended to make him "hit the dust" or jump out of the way to avoid being hit by the pitch.

EARNED RUN—A run scored without the aid of an error or passed ball.

EARNED-RUN AVERAGE (ERA)—The average number of earned runs scored against a pitcher for every nine innings he pitches; the average is obtained by dividing the total number of earned runs by the number of innings pitched and multiplying this figure by nine. A low ERA is preferred.

ERROR—A misplay of a ball by a fielder.

EVEN THE COUNT—A situation where a batter or pitcher is able to get the count even—that is, a like number of balls and strikes.

EXTRA-BASE-HIT—Any hit other than a single.

EXTRA INNING—Any inning beyond the regulation nine.

FAIR BALL—A ball that is in play.

FAIR TERRITORY—The area between the foul lines that makes up the playing field's fair-ball territory.

FAN—To strike out (WHIFF).

FASTBALL—A pitch thrown with power and speed.

FIELD—The handling of a batted ball by a defensive player.

FIELDER—A defensive player other than the catcher or pitcher.

FIELDER'S CHOICE—A situation where a fielder, after gaining possession of a batted ball, can elect either to throw out the batter who is running to first base or to attempt to throw out another base runner. A batter who reaches base because the fielder elected to go after the base runner is credited with reaching base on a fielder's choice. A time at bat is charged to the batter.

FIELDING AVERAGE—The percentage of chances fielded successfully versus errors committed, which reveals a player's defensive skills, at least from a statistical point of view.

FIREBALL—A fastball-throwing pitcher (HARD CHUCKER; FLAME THROWER).

FIREMAN—A relief pitcher.

FIRST—Refers to first base.

FIRST BASEMAN—A player whose position is first base (FIRST SACKER).

FLY—A batted ball hit high in the air (FLY BALL).

FORCE OUT—The retiring of a runner on a force play.

FORCE PLAY—A condition where a runner must leave his base and move to the next base because of a ground ball the batter has hit. The runner's failure to reach the next base before it is touched by a defensive player in possession of the ball creates a force out.

FOUL BALL—A ball hit into foul territory.

FOUL LINES—The boundry lines of fair territory that extend on a right angle from the back corner of home plate past the outside edges of first and third base and on into the outfield.

FOUL OFF—To hit a pitched ball foul.

FOUL OUT—To foul off a pitch and have it caught by a defensive player before it touches the ground for an out.

FOUL POLES—Vertical extensions of the foul lines whose lower portions are generally painted on the outfield walls, above which extends the actual pole.

FOUL TERRITORY—The opposite of fair territory.

FOUL TIP—A ball swung at and tipped back by the batter and then caught by the catcher.

FOUR-BAGGER—A home run (CIRCUIT CLOUT).

FULL COUNT—Three balls and two strikes on a batter.

FUMBLE—To bobble a ground ball.

GOPHER BALL—A pitch that "goes for" a home run—not a very well-thrown pitch from the pitcher's point of view.

GO WITH THE PITCH—To hit the ball where it is pitched and not to attempt to overpower it.

GRANDSLAMMER—A bases-loaded home run.

GROOVE—To throw a pitch over the fat, middle part of the plate. To be in a good, flowing playing condition, such as a batting groove.

GROUNDER—A ball that is hit along the ground.

GROUNDOUT—To be retired at first base on a grounder to an infielder.

GROUND OUT—To hit into a groundout.

GROUND RULE—A special rule governing the course of play that is put into effect because of the particular features of a ball park.

GROUND-RULE DOUBLE—The awarding of two bases (a double) to a batter who hits a ball into a special ground-rule situation—the batted ball, for example, bouncing into the stands.

HIGH PITCH—A pitch that is above the batter's strike zone.

HIT AND RUN—A play in which the batter swings at the ball and the runner on base breaks for the next base.

HIT THE DIRT—A situation in which a batter drops to the ground to avoid being hit by a pitched ball or where a base runner jumps back to the base to avoid being picked off by the pitcher.

HOLD ON BASE—A condition in which a pitcher, by keeping an eye on the runner and sometimes throwing the ball to the defender stationed at that base, attempts to keep the runner from taking too big a lead or stealing a base.

HOME—A short way of saying home plate.

HOME PLATE—A slab of white rubber with five sides that the pitcher throws to; it is the final base touched by a runner to score a run.

HOME RUN—A hit that leaves the ball park in fair territory; it is worth one run, or more if there are men on base. The batter is allowed to trot around the bases uncontested (FOUR BAGGER; CIRCUIT CLOUT).

HURL—To pitch (CHUCK).

HURLER—A pitcher (CHUCKER).

INFIELDER—The position of first baseman, second baseman, third baseman, and shortstop.

INFIELD FLY—A situation that occurs when, with less than two men out and with either all three bases occupied or first and second bases occupied, a hitter pops the ball up to the infield; the hitter is automatically declared out and the runners may advance at their own risk.

INFIELD HIT—A hit achieved by hitting a ball that does not leave the infield.

INFIELD OUT—The retiring of a batter on a ball hit in the infield.

INNING—A period of play that consists of three outs for each team. A regulation game consists of nine innings.

INSIDE-THE-PARK HOME RUN—A home run that takes place when the ball is hit and is in play and the batter is able to reach home plate before being tagged out.

INTENTIONAL WALK—A situation in which a pitcher deliberately throws four balls to a batter in a strategic attempt to prevent the batter from hitting.

INTERFERENCE—Getting in the way of a runner, a fielder, or hitter and making it difficult for that player to perform unhindered action.

K—The scorecard symbol for a strikeout.

KEYSTONE—Second base.

KEYSTONE COMBINATION—The second baseman and the shortstop.

KNOCK OUT OF THE BOX—To score runs against a pitcher in such a way that he is removed from the game.

KNUCKLEBALL—An unusual pitch that flutters as it comes to the batter (FLUTTERBALL; KNUCKLER).

KNUCKLE CURVE—A combination knuckleball and curveball.

LAY DOWN A BUNT—The act of bunting the ball.

LEAD—The amount of steps a base runner takes off a base. A short lead takes place when the runner is close to the base. A long lead describes a proportionately longer distance off the base.

LEADOFF BATTER (MAN)—The first hitter in the team's lineup or in an inning.

LEAD OFF—To bat first in an inning or in the team's lineup.

LEAVE MEN ON BASE—A situation at the end of an inning when a team has been retired and one or more base runners have been left on base, unable to score (STRAND BASE RUNNER[S]).

LEFT FIELD—Viewed from home plate, the left side of the outfield.

LEG HIT—A base hit awarded to a runner who beats out a ground ball to the infield by using his speed.

LINE OUT—To hit a line drive that is caught for an out.

LINE—A ball hit straight and solidly (LINE DRIVE).

LINE SCORE—A printed summary account, inning by inning, of a game.

LIVE BALL—A ball that, because of its alleged composition, will travel a long way when hit—as opposed to a dead ball (RABBIT BALL).

LOAD THE BALL—The illegal placement by a pitcher of saliva or some other foreign subtance on the ball, to gain an edge by causing the ball to move about unpredictably.

LOAD THE BASES—An offensive team's placing of runners on each base (BASES FULL).

LONG-BALL HITTER—A batter who hits the ball for distance.

LOOPER—A batted ball that drops in flight.

LOSING PITCHER—The pitcher who is officially charged with a loss.

LOW PITCH—A pitch that comes in below the strike zone.

MOUND—A raised surface in the center of the diamond on which the pitcher stands and throws to the batter.

MOUNDSMAN—Another name for a pitcher.

NAIL—The act of throwing out a runner.

NINE—A baseball team (STARTING NINE).

NO-HITTER—A game in which a pitcher (or pitchers) on one team does not allow any hits to the opposition.

OFFICIAL GAME—A game that goes 4½ innings with home team ahead or five innings with visitors leading.

OFFICIAL SCORER—The person who records the score and statistics of a game and rules on whether a hit or an error, etc., should be charged to a player on a particular situation.

OFF-SPEED PITCH—A pitch that is slower than others a pitcher usually throws, so that the difference in velocity affects the timing of a hitter.

ON DECK—A term describing a player stationed in the batter's on-deck circle in front of the dugout, preparing to be the next batter to come up and hit.

ONE-BAGGER (ONE-BASE HIT)—A single.

OUT—To be retired by the defense.

OUTFIELD—The playing area beyond the infield where outfielders are stationed.

OUTFIELDER—The positions of left fielder, right fielder, and center fielder (PICKETMAN).

OUTHIT—To get more hits than another player or team.

OUTPITCH—To pitch better than an opponent.

OUTSLUG—Usually, to defeat another team by displaying more extra-base power.

OVERSLIDE—To slide into a base and then past it.

PENNANT—A pennant-shaped banner that symbolizes the winning of a league championship (FLAG).

PENNANT RACE—The battle for the pennant among contending teams.

PERCENTAGE PLAYER OR MANAGER—One who goes by past form or logical odds and acts on the basis of these conditions.

PERFECT GAME—A no-hitter in which all 27 opposing batters in a nine-inning game, for example, are not allowed to get on base.

PILOT—Another name for a baseball manager. To manage a team.

PINCH HIT—To come up to the plate to hit for another batter.

PINCH HITTER—The player who comes up to the plate to hit for another batter.

PINCH RUN—To function as a substitute runner for another player. The substitute takes the other player's place at the base that the player had occupied.

PINCH RUNNER—A generally faster runner who comes into a game to take the place of a man on base and to run for him.

PITCH—To throw the ball to the batter from the pitcher's mound.

PITCHER—The player who is positioned on the pitcher's mound who throws the ball to the plate (HURLER; MOUNDSMAN; CHUCKER; TWIRLER).

PITCHER-OF-RECORD—A pitcher officially liable to be charged with a win or loss even though he has been removed from a game. This condition prevails until or unless the score is tied and a new pitcher-of-record is established.

PITCHER'S MOUND—Located on a line between home plate and second base, this raised surface is the area a pitcher operates from.

PIVOT—A second baseman's turning maneuver as he touches the base with one foot and whirls about to throw to first base to complete a double-play attempt.

PLATE UMPIRE—The home-plate umpire.

PLAYOFFS—Postseason competition to determine league entry into World Series.

POP FLY, POP IT UP, POP-UP, POP—All signify a short fly ball.

POP-FOUL—To hit a short, foul fly ball.

POP OUT—To be retired on a short fly ball.

POPPING THE BALL—The act of a pitcher throwing the ball so hard at the catcher that it can be heard "popping" into the catcher's mitt.

POTENTIAL TYING RUN—A base runner or a hitter who, if he eventaully scores, will tie the game up. Thus, each time a team losing by one run gets a man on base or to the plate, that player is the potential tying run.

POWER ALLEY—An area in the outfield that a particular player can hit to with power; the areas between center field and right field, and centerfield and left field where many home runs are hit.

PROTECT THE PLATE—The defensive behaviour of a batter swinging at pitches that he thinks may be called strikes.

PROTECT THE RUNNER—The act of a hitter swinging at any pitch in a hit-and-run or steal situation to attempt to hamper a catcher's throw aimed at putting out the runner.

PUTOUT—The actual act of retiring a player, the first baseman who catches the ball thrown by a shortstop to retire the runner streaking down the first-base line gets credit for a putout, for example.

RABBIT BALL—A lively baseball; one that can be hit for distance.

RACK CHECK—That portion of the ticket that permits a fan to attend another game in place of one that has been rained out.

RAIN DATE—The alternate date for a game that was rained out.

RAIN DELAY—The interrupton of a game because of rain; the game may be continued if the rain lets up.

RAINOUT—A game that is called because of rain (WASHOUT).

RBI—Abbreviation for a run batted in (RIBBY).

RELIEF PITCHER—A pitcher who comes in to take the place of another pitcher on his team who is not hurling effectively or who has gotten injured or tired (RELIEF; RELIEVER).

RETIRE THE SIDE IN ORDER—The act of a pitcher facing only three batters, none of whom does he allow to get to first base.

RHUBARB—A passionate difference of opinion that produces an extended argument on the playing field.

RIDE THE BENCH—A phrase that describes a substitute who sits on the bench in the dugout.

RIGHT-CENTER FIELD—The area between right field and center field.

RIGHT FIELD—Looking from home plate, the part of the outfield on the right side.

ROSIN BAG—A pouch with powdered rosin used by pitchers to keep their throwing hand dry.

ROUNDHOUSE CURVE—A pitch that breaks wide and slow.

ROUND THE BASES—To trot around the bases, touching each one, after hitting a home run.

ROUND TRIPPER—A home run (CIRCUIT CLOUT; FOUR BAGGER).

RUBBER-The white rubber slat positioned on the pitcher's mound, the front edge of which is 60½ feet from home plate. The pitcher cannot throw to home unless his foot is in contact with this object, or else a balk is called.

RUBBER-ARMED PITCHER—A pitcher, usually a relief pitcher, who is capable of pitching often and long and whose arm does not reflect the stress and strain of hard work.

RUN—A score of one run is made each time a player crosses home plate (TALLY; MARKER; SCORE).

RUN AND HIT—A situation where a player on base runs and then the batter at the plate hits.

RUNDOWN—A situation where a player is trapped between two bases and is chased back and forth by the defenders as he attempts to wind up safely on one of the bases.

SACK—Base (BAG).

SACRIFICE—A bunted ball that advances a teammate, or a ball hit to the outfield that enables a runner to tag up and score. The player committing the sacrifice does not reach base, but he also does not get a time at bat charged against his batting average (SACRIFICE BUNT: SACRIFICE HIT; SACRIFICE FLY).

SAFETY—Base hit, bingle.

SCORE—The amount of runs each team achieves or is achieving at a given moment in a game. To drive in a run. To cross the plate and tally a run.

SCOREBOARD—A highly visible board, generally beyond the out-field, that gives information about the score, the batting orders, the pitchers, other games in progress, or scheduled coming events.

SCORECARD—A program purchased at ball park by fans, who use it to keep score of the game in progress.

SCORING POSITION—Location on the bases (generally second or third) from which a player can score on a hit or a fly ball.

SCREEN—A wire barrier covering the area in the stands behind home plate to prevent fans from being hit by foul balls.

SCREWBALL—A seemingly straight pitch which unexpectedly swerves to the right (when thrown by a right-handed pitcher) or to the left (when thrown by a left-handed pitcher) (SCROOGIE).

SECOND BASE—The base midway between first base and third base and lined up with home plate (SECOND).

SECOND BASEMAN—A fielder positioned, as a rule, to the right of second base. This player is a key man in double plays and in covering the area around his position and between first and second base.

SET DOWN IN ORDER—To retire a side in order with no hits, no walks, no errors, and no runs.

SET POSITION—A pitcher's stance assumed after a stretch—the ball is held in front of the body, with one foot positioned on the rubber.

SEVENTH-INNING STRETCH—A baseball custom that enables fans to stand and to stretch a few moments before the second half of the seventh inning.

SHAKE OFF A SIGN—A situation where a pitcher will not accept a sign for a pitch given by a catcher and will indicate this by head or glove movement.

SHIFT—To move players from traditional defensive positions to other locations to compensate for a hitter's pattern.

SHOESTRING CATCH—The grabbing of a fly ball by an outfielder just as it is about to hit the ground.

SHORTEN UP THE INFIELD—A defensive move in which infielders move in closer to the plate.

SHORT-HOP—To grab a batted ball by charging in at it and seizing it before it bounces high.

SHORT RELIEVER—A relief pitcher who pitches for a brief time (SHORT RELIEF; SPOT RELIEVER; SHORT MAN).

SHORTSTOP—A player positioned between third base and second base, closer to second, who has double-play responsibilities as a main part of his job.

SHOT—A hard-hit ball.

SHUTOUT—A game in which a pitcher holds the opposition scoreless.

SIDEARMER—A pitcher who throws the ball to the plate from a sidearm position, as opposed to overhanded.

SINGLE—A one-base hit.

SINGLE IN A RUN—To score a runner by hitting a single.

SINKER—A pitch that drops as it nears the plate.

SINKING LINER—A line drive that drops as it gathers distance.

SKIMMER—A batted ball that rapidly glides across the ground.

SLIDE—The action of a base runner hitting the ground and coming into a base head- or feet-first. A belly slide is a variation in which a player flops on his belly with hands outstretched toward the base.

SLUGGER—A player who gets long extra-base hits.

SLUGGING AVERAGE—The ratio of total bases achieved to number of times at bat, which indicates the extra-base capability of the batter.

SLUMP—A period of ineffectiveness for a team or an individual.

SMASH—A powerfully hit ball.

SOLID CONTACT—The act of hitting the ball and getting "good wood" or the fat part of the bat into contact with the ball.

SOLO CLOUT—A home run with no one on base.

SOUTHPAW—A left-handed pitcher.

SPIKE—To inflict injury on another player with the spikes on baseball shoes—in sliding situations, for example.

SPIKES—Metal projections on the bottom of the shoes worn by baseball players.

SPITTER—An illegal pitch that involves a pitcher placing saliva or some other moist substance on the ball to make it break oddly as it comes to the batter (SPITBALL; MOIST PITCH; WET PITCH).

SPOT STARTER—A pitcher called into action to start games as the team needs him, as opposed to a regular starting pitcher.

SPRING TRAINING—The conditioning and exhibition season of professional baseball teams, which generally starts in late February in a warm-weather climate and lasts until a few days before the start of the new season.

SQUARE AROUND TO BUNT—A batter's movement out of a normal batting stance into a position facing the pitcher, with the bat extended parallel to the batter's feet, which point toward the infield.

SQUEEZE PLAY—An offensive strategy move in which a team with less than two outs and a man on third base will have a batter bunt the ball, hoping the runner will be able to score. A SAFETY SQUEEZE takes place when the runner waits to see how effective the bunt is. A SUICIDE SQUEEZE takes place when the runner breaks the instant the pitch is released.

START—An opportunity given to a pitcher to begin a game. To be the pitcher who begins a game.

STARTER—A pitcher who starts a game (STARTING PITCHER).

STARTING ROTATION—The order in which starting pitchers perform on a daily basis—every fourth or fifth day as a starter is the general rule, which would mean that a team has four or five starters.

STEAL—To run from one base to the next, attempting to get there safely by catching the other team off guard.

STEP UP TO THE PLATE—To get into the batter's box in preparation to hit.

STOLEN BASE—A successful steal of a base by a runner.

STOP—To bring a batted ball under control by knocking it down or slowing its movement so as to be able to play it.

STRANDED—A term that describes a runner or runners left on base at the end of an inning, unable to be brought into score by other hitters on their team (LEFT ON BASE).

STRIKE—A pitch in the strike zone or one that is swung at and missed or fouled off. A highly accurate outfielder's throw.

STRIKEOUT—The act of retiring a batter by getting three strikes on him.

STRIKE OUT—The act of a batter being out on strikes.

STRIKE ZONE—The imaginary area that extends over home plate from the batter's knees to his armpits; a pitch thrown in the strike zone will be a strike on the batter unless he hits it into fair territory.

SWAT THE BALL—To hit the ball with power and for distance.

SWEEP A SERIES—To win all the games in a series played with another team.

SWING—To move the bat in an arced motion to hit a pitched ball.

SWING AWAY—To take a full cut (full swing) at a pitch.

SWINGING BUNT—A half swing, half bunt.

SWITCH HITTER—A batter who can hit from either side of the plate.

TAB—To select a player for a certain performance—to "tab a pitcher to start the first game of the World Series."

TAG OUT—To touch a base runner with the ball as he is off base, thus making him out (TAG).

TAG UP—A situation where a runner stays on base until a fly ball is caught and then has the option to run to the next base, attempting to beat the throw.

TAKE A PITCH—To allow a pitch to come over the plate without swinging at it.

TAKE OFF—The opening move in the running of a player from one base to another in an attempt to steal a base. A condition where a pitch suddenly deviates in its motion as it comes to the plate (usually refers to a ball that rises sharply).

TAKE-OUT PLAY—A situation where a base runner slides into a fielder, attempting to off-balance that player and prevent his making a play.

TAKE SIGN—A signal from a manager or coach to a batter to not swing at a pitch.

THIRD BASE—The base on the left side of the infield, as viewed from home plate (THIRD).

THIRD BASEMAN—The player whose position is third base and who defensively covers mainly the area between third and shortstop (THIRD SACKER; HOT SACK GUARDIAN).

THREE-BASE HIT—A triple (THREE-BAGGER).

THREE-HUNDRED HITTER—A batter who hits .300 or better.

THROWER—A pitcher not distinguished by his thinking ability.

THROW OUT A BALL—A situation where an umpire discards a ball that has become not playable because it is scuffed, marked, or dirtied.

THROW OUT A RUNNER—The act of throwing a ball to a fielder who tags out a base runner.

TOP—The first half of an inning. To hit a ball above its center line so that its flight or roll has topspin.

TOTAL BASES—The adding up of the number of bases a hit is equal to: a single is one base, a double is two bases, a triple is three bases, a home run is four bases.

TRACK IT DOWN—The running after and catching of a flyball by an outfielder.

TRIPLE—A three-base hit (THREE-BAGGER).

TRIPLE CROWN—The winning of the batting championship, home run title, and RBI crown by one player in the same season.

TRIPLE PLAY—Three outs recorded on one play.

TWIN BILL—A doubleheader.

TWIN-NIGHT DOUBLEHEADER—Two games, usually for the same admission charge; the first game takes place in early evening and the second game immediately follows.

TWO-BASE HIT—A double (TWO-BAGGER).

UMPIRES—Personnel who officiate at a game: the home plate umpire is stationed behind the plate and calls balls and strikes; other umpires are stationed near each base (ARBITERS; MEN IN BLUE; UMPS).

UNEARNED RUN—A run scored as a result of a mistake made by the defensive team and not charged against a pitcher's earned-run average.

VELOCITY—The speed of a pitched ball (ZIP).

WALK—The receiving of a fourth pitch outside the strike zone by a batter, which allows him to move to first base (PASS; BASE ON BALLS).

WARMING UP—The throwing of practice pitches in the bullpen by a relief pitcher who is readying himself to enter the game.

WARM-UP PITCHES—Practice pitches allowed a pitcher each inning before the opposing side comes up to bat.

WASTED PITCH—A ball intentionally pitched out of the strike zone to get the batter to swing at it or set him up for the next pitch.

WHITEWASH—To shut out a team (BLANK).

WIDE—A pitch outside the strike zone.

WIDE PITCH—A pitch far outside the strike zone that cannot be handled by the catcher.

WILD THROW—A throw to a defensive player that is so inaccurate that it can't be handled.

WINDUP—Arm and leg motions by a pitcher that serve as preliminary steps for the pitching of a ball.

WINNING PITCHER—A pitcher officially given credit for a victory.

WINTER BALL—Off-season, warm weather baseball competition.

WORLD SERIES—The seven-game postseason championship between the winners of the National League and the American League pennants. The first team to win four games is declared the world champion.

WRIST HITTER—A player who gets good wrist action into his swing at a ball.

KEEPING YOUR GAMING
KNOWLEDGE CURRENT

Now that you know how to beat the propositions in the casino, the sports book, and at the track, it's important to keep abreast of the rapid and continuous changes and developments in these areas. The best way to do that is with a subscription to *Gambling Times* magazine.

Since February of 1977, readers of *Gambling Times* magazine have profited immensely. They have done so by using the information they have read each month. If that sounds like a simple solution to winning more and losing less, well it is! Readers look to *Gambling Times* for that very specific reason. And it delivers.

Gambling Times is totally dedicated to showing readers how to win more money in every form of legalized gambling. How much you're going to win depends on many factors, but it's going to be considerably more than the cost of a subscription.

WINNING AND MONEY

Winning, that's what *Gambling Times* is all about. And money, that's what *Gambling Times* is all about. Because winning and money go hand in hand.

Here's what the late Vince Lombardi, the famous football coach of the Green Bay Packers, had to say about winning:

> "It's not a sometime thing. Winning is a habit. There is no room for second place. There is only one place in my game and that is first place. I have finished second twice in my time at Green Bay and I don't ever want to finish second again. The objective is to win—fairly, squarely, decently, by the rules—but to win. To beat the other guy. Maybe that sounds hard or cruel. I don't think it is. It is and has always been an American zeal to be first in anything we do, and to win, and to win and to win."

Mr. Lombardi firmly believed that being a winner is "man's finest hour." *Gambling Times* believes it is too, while being a loser is depressing, ego-deflating, expensive and usually very lonely. "Everybody loves a winner" may be a cliche, but it's true. Winners command respect and are greatly admired. Winners are also very popular and have an abundance of friends. You may have seen a winner in a casino, with a bevy of girls surrounding him...or remember one who could get just about any girl he wanted.

Some of the greatest gamblers in the world also have strong views on what winning is all about. Here's what two of them have to say on the subject:

"To be a winner, a man has to feel good about himself and know he has some kind of advantage going in. I never made bets on even chances. Smart is better than lucky."— "Titanic" Thompson

"When it comes to winnin', I got me a one-track mind. You gotta want to win more than anything else. And you gotta have confidence. You can't pretend to have it. That's no good. You gotta have it. You gotta know. Guessers are losers. Gamblin's just as simple as that."—Johnny Moss

Gambling Times will bring you the knowledge you need to come home a winner and come home in the money. For it is knowledge, the kind of knowledge you'll get in its pages, that separates winners from losers. It's winning and money that *Gambling Times* offers you. *Gambling Times* will be your working manual to winning wealth.

The current distribution of this magazine is limited to selected newsstands in selected cities. Additionally, at newsstands where it is available, it's being snapped up, as soon as it's displayed, by gamblers who know a sure bet when they see one.

So if you're serious about winning, you're best off subscribing to *Gambling Times*. Then you can always count on its being there, conveniently delivered to your mailbox—and what's more, it will be there one to two weeks before it appears on the newsstands. You'll be among the first to receive the current issue as soon as it comes off the presses, and being first is the way to be a winner.

Having every monthly issue of *Gambling Times* will enable you to build an "Encyclopedia of Gambling," since the contents of this magazine are full of sound advice that will be as good in five or ten years as it is now.

As you can see, a subscription to *Gambling Times* is your best bet for a future of knowledgeable gambling. It's your ticket to *WINNING* and *MONEY.*

Take the time to read the following offer. As you can see, *Gambling Times* has gone all out to give you outstanding bonuses. You can join the knowledgeable players who have learned that *Gambling Times* helps them to win more money.

FOUR NEW WAYS TO GET 12 WINNING ISSUES OF *GAMBLING TIMES* FREE...

Every month over 250,000 readers trust *Gambling Times* to introduce powerful new winning strategies and systems. Using proven scientific methods, the world's leading experts show you how to win big money in the complex field of gambling.

Gambling Times has shown how progressive slot machines can be beat. Readers have discovered important new edges in blackjack. They've been shown how to know for sure when an opponent is bluffing at poker. *Gambling Times* has also spelled out winning methods for football, baseball and basketball. They've published profound new ways of beating horses. Their team of experts will uncover information in the months ahead that's certain to be worth thousands of dollars to you.

In fact, the features are so revolutionary that they must take special precautions to make sure *Gambling Times* readers learn these secrets long before anyone else. So how much is *Gambling Times* worth to you? Well...

NOW *GAMBLING TIMES* CAN BE BETTER THAN FREE! Here's how: This BONUS package comes AUTOMATICALLY TO YOU WHEN YOU SUBSCRIBE...or goes to a friend if you give a gift subscription.

(1)   POKER BONUS at the TROPICANA card room in Las Vegas.

Play poker at the TROPICANA and receive a free dinner buffet and comps to the "Folies Bergere" show for you *and* a guest. Value exceeds $40 excluding gratuities.

(2) FREE SPORTS BET. CHURCHILL DOWNS SPORTS BOOK in Las Vegas will let you make one wager up to $300 with no "vigorish." This means instead of laying the usual 11-to-10 odds, you can actually bet even up! You can easily save $30 here.

(3) PAYOFF BIGGER THAN THE TRACK. LEROY'S RACE BOOK, in Las Vegas, will add 10% to your payoff (up to $30 extra) on a special bet. Just pick the horse and the race of your choice, anywhere in America. For the first time in history, you can win more than the track pays.

(4) OUTSTANDING ROOM DISCOUNTS available only to *Gambling Times* subscribers. Check in at the SANDS in Las Vegas or Atlantic City, the TROPICANA in Atlantic City, the HIGH SIERRA in Lake Tahoe, or the CONDADO INN & CASINO in San Juan, Puerto Rico. Stay for 3 days and 2 nights and you'll save $29 off their normal low rates.

THAT'S A SAVING GREATER THAN THE ENTIRE COST OF YOUR SUBSCRIPTION.

USE ALL FOUR CERTIFICATES (VALID FOR ONE YEAR)...GET *GAMBLING TIMES* FREE...AND YOU'LL PUT $93 IN YOUR POCKET!

To begin your delivery of *Gambling Times* magazine at once, enclose a payment of $36.00 by check or money order (U.S. currency), MasterCard or Visa. Add $5.00 per year for postage outside the United States.

Send payment to:

GAMBLING TIMES MAGAZINE
1018 N. Cole Avenue
Hollywood, California 90038

GAMBLING TIMES
MONEY BACK GUARANTEE

If at any time you decide *Gambling Times* is not for you, you will receive a full refund on all unmailed copies. You are under no obligation and may keep the bonus as a gift.

Other Valuable Sources of Knowledge Available Through *Gambling Times*

(See ordering information on page 176.)

Here are some additional sources you can turn to for worthwhile gambling information:

The Experts Sports Handicapping Newsletter

Published monthly, this newsletter will show you how to become an Expert handicapper. You will learn the different styles of handicapping and be able to select the one method best suited to your personality. Yearly subscriptions are $60; $50 for *Gambling Times* subscribers.

The Experts Blackjack Newsletter

This monthly newsletter has all the top blackjack Experts working just for you. Features answers, strategies and insights that were never before possible. Yearly subscriptions are $60; $50 for *Gambling Times* subscribers.

Poker Player

Published every other week, this *Gambling Times* newspaper features the best writers and theorists on the poker scene today. You will learn all aspects of poker, from odds to psychology, as well as how to play in no-limit competition and in tournaments. Yearly subscriptions (26 issues) are $20.

OTHER BOOKS AVAILABLE

If you can't find the following books at your local bookstore, they may be ordered directly from *Gambling Times,* 1018 N. Cole Ave., Hollywood, CA 90038. Information on how to order is on page 176.

Poker Books

According to Doyle by Doyle Brunson—Acknowledged by most people as the world's best all-around poker player, twice World Champion Doyle Brunson brings you his homespun wisdom from over 30 years as a professional poker player. This book will not only show you how to win at poker, it will give you valuable insights into how to better handle that poker game called LIFE.
Softbound. $6.95. (ISBN: 0-89746-003-0)

Caro on Gambling by Mike Caro—The world's leading poker writer covers all the aspects of gambling from his regular columns in *Gambling Times* magazine and *Poker Player* newspaper. Discussing odds and probabilities, bluffing and raising, psychology and character, this book will bring to light valuable concepts that can be turned into instant profits in home games as well as in the poker palaces of the West.
Softbound. $6.95. (ISBN: 0-89746-029-4)

Caro's Book of Tells by Mike Caro—The photographic body language of poker. Approximately 150 photographs with text explaining when a player is bluffing, when he's got the winning hand—and WHY. Based on accurate investigation; it is NOT guesswork. Even the greatest of gamblers has some giveaway behavior. For the first time in print, one of the world's top poker players reveals how he virtually can read minds because nearly every player has a "tell." Seal the leaks in your poker game and empty your opponent's chip tray.
Hardbound. $20.00. (ISBN: 0-914314-04-1)

The Gambling Times Official Rules of Poker by Mike Caro—Settles home poker arguments. Caro has written the revised rule book (including a section on etiquette) for the Horseshoe Club in Gardena, California, that may soon be adopted by other clubs and become the California standard. He is presently scheduling a meeting of poker room managers

at the Bingo Palace in Las Vegas. This should lead to the creation of a uniform book of rules for Nevada cardrooms. *The Gambling Times Official Rules of Poker* includes sections of the rules from public cardrooms, but mostly it is for home poker. The book is needed because there presently exists no true authority for settling Friday night poker disputes.
Softbound. $5.95. (ISBN: 0-89746-012-X)

Poker for Women by Mike Caro—How women can take advantage of the special male-female ego wars at the poker table and win. This book also has non-poker everyday value for women. Men can be destroyed at the poker table by coy, cunning or aggressive women. That's because, on a subconscious level, men expect women to act traditionally. This book tells women when to flirt, when to be tough and when to whimper. Many of the tactics are tried and proven by Caro's own students. This book does not claim that women are better players, merely that there are strategies available to them that are not available to their male opponents.
Softbound. $5.95. (ISBN: 0-89746-009-X)

Poker Without Cards by Mike Caro—Applying world-class poker tactics to everyday life. Is the salesman bluffing? Can you get a better price? Negotiating is like playing a poker hand. Although poker tactics are common in daily encounters, few people realize when a hand is being played. It's hard to make the right decision when you're not even aware that you've been raised. The book is honest and accurate in its evaluation of behavior.
Softbound. $6.95. (ISBN: 0-89746-038-3)

Win, Places, and Pros by Tex Sheahan—With more than 50 years of experience as a professional poker player and cardroom manager/tournament director, Tex lets his readers in on the secrets that separate the men from the boys at the poker table. Descriptions of poker events, playing experiences from all over the world, and those special personalities who are the masters of the game. . .Tex knows them all and lays it out in his marvelous easy-to-read style.
Softbound. $6.95. (ISBN: 0-89746-008-1)

Blackjack Books

The Beginner's Guide to Winning Blackjack by Stanley Roberts—The world's leading blackjack writer shows beginners to the game how to obtain an instant advantage through the simplest of techniques. Covering Basic Strategy for all major casino areas from Las Vegas to the Bahamas, Atlantic City and Reno/Tahoe, Roberts provides a simple system to immediately know when the remaining cards favor the player. The entire method can be learned in less than two hours and taken to the casinos to produce sure profits.
Softbound. $10.00. (ISBN: 0-89746-014-6)

The Gambling Times Guide to Blackjack by Stanley Roberts with Edward O. Thorp, Ken Uston, Lance Humble, Arnold Snyder, Julian Braun, Richard Canfield and other experts in this field—The top blackjack authorities have been brought together for the first time to bring to the reader the ins and outs of the game of blackjack. All aspects of the game are discussed. Winning techniques are presented for beginners and casual players.
Softbound. $5.95. (ISBN: 0-89746-015-4)

Million Dollar Blackjack by Ken Uston—Every blackjack enthusiast or gaming traveler who fancies himself a "21" player can improve his game with this explosive bestseller. Ken Uston shows you how he and his team won over 4 million dollars at blackjack. Now, for the first time, you can find out how he did it and how his system can help you. Includes playing and betting strategies, winning secrets, protection from cheaters, Uston's Advanced Point Count System, and a glossary of inside terms used by professionals. More than 50,000 copies in print.
Hardbound. $18.95. (ISBN: 0-914314-08-4)

Casino Games

The Gambling Times Guide to Casino Games by Len Miller—The co-founder and editor of *Gambling Times* magazine vividly describes the casino games and explains their rules and betting procedures. This easy-to-follow guide covers blackjack, craps, roulette, keno, video machines, progressive slots and more. After reading this book, you'll play like a pro!
Softbound. $5.95. (ISBN: 0-89746-017-0)

The Gambling Times Guide to Craps by N.B. Winkless, Jr.—The ultimate craps book for beginners and experts alike. It provides you with a program to tackle the house edge that can be used on a home computer. This text shows you which bets to avoid and tells you the difference between craps in Nevada and craps in other gaming resort areas. It includes a glossary of terms and a directory of dealer schools. Softbound. $5.95. (ISBN: 0-89746-013-8)

General Interest Books

According to Gambling Times: The Rules of Gambling Games by Stanley Roberts—At last you can finally settle all the arguments regarding what the rules are in every known gambling endeavor. From pari-mutuels to bookie slips, from blackjack to gin rummy, the rules of the games and the variations that are generally accepted in both public and private situations are clearly enumerated by the world's #1 gaming authority. Hardbound. $12.00. (ISBN: 0-914314-07-6)

The Gambling Times Guide to Gaming Around the World compiled by Arnold L. Abrams—The complete travel guide to legal gaming throughout the world. This comprehensive gaming guide lists casinos around the world; the games played in each; cardrooms and facilities; greyhound racing and horse racing tracks, as well as jai alai frontons, lotteries and sports betting facilities. This book is a must for the traveling gamer. Softbound. $5.95. (ISBN: 0-89746-020-0)

The Gambling Times Guide to Systems That Win, Volume I—For those who want to broaden their gambling knowledge, this book offers complete gambling systems used by the experts. Learn their strategies and how to incorporate them into your gambling style. **Volume I** covers 12 systems that win for roulette, craps, backgammon, slot machines, horse racing, baseball, basketball and football. Softbound. $5.95. (ISBN: 0-89746-034-0)

The Gambling Times Guide to Winning Systems, Volume I and Volume II—For those who take their gambling seriously, *Gambling Times* presents a two-volume set of proven winning systems. Learn how the experts beat the house edge and become consistent winners. **Volume I** contains 12 complete strategies for casino games and sports wagering, including baccarat, blackjack, keno, basketball and harness handicapping.
Softbound. $5.95. (ISBN: 0-89746-032-4)
Volume II contains 12 more winning systems covering poker bluffing, pitching analysis, greyhound handicapping and roulette.
Softbound. $5.95. (ISBN: 0-89746-033-2)

Gambling Times Presents Winning Systems and Methods, Volume I and Volume II—This two-volume collection of winning strategies by some of the nation's leading experts on gambling will help you in your quest to beat the percentages. **Volume I** includes several chapters on blackjack, as well as methods for beating baseball, basketball, hockey, steeplechase and grass racing.
Softbound. $5.95. (ISBN: 0-89746-036-7)
Volume II contains an analysis of keno and video poker, as well as systems for success in sports betting and horse racing.
Softbound. $5.95. (ISBN: 0-89746-037-5)

The Mathematics of Gambling by Edward O. Thorp—The "Albert Einstein of gambling" presents his second book on the subject. His first book, *Beat The Dealer,* set the gambling world on its heels and struck fear into the cold-blooded hearts of Las Vegas casino-owners in 1962. Now, more than twenty years later, Dr. Thorp again challenges the odds by bringing out a simple to understand version of more than thirty years of exploration into all aspects of what separates winners from losers...knowing the real meaning of the parameters of the games.
Softbound. $7.95. (ISBN: 0-89746-019-7)

Odds: Quick and Simple by Mike Caro—How to know the right lines and win by figuring the odds logically. Common sense replaces mathematical formulas. This book will teach probabilities plainly and powerfully. The emphasis will be on gambling, showing how to quickly determine whether or not to make a wager. Particular emphasis will be on sports bets, pot odds in poker, dice and various proposition bets. Also

included will be tables of the most important gambling odds (craps, roulette, poker, blackjack, keno) for easy reference.
Softbound. $5.95. (ISBN: 0-89746-030-8)

P$yching Out Vegas by Marvin Karlins, Ph.D.—The dream merchants who build and operate gaming resorts subtly work on the casino patron to direct his attention, control his actions and turn his pockets inside out. At last, their techniques are revealed to you by a noted psychologist who shows you how you can successfully control your behavior and turn a losing attitude into a lifetime winning streak.
Hardbound. $12.00. (ISBN: 0-914314-03-3)

Winning by Computer by Dr. Donald Sullivan—Now, for the first time, the wonders of computer technology are harnessed for the gambler. Dr. Sullivan explains how to figure the odds and identify key factors in all forms of race and sports handicapping.
Softbound. $5.95. (ISBN: 0-89746-018-9)

Sports Betting Books

The Gambling Times Guide to Basketball Handicapping by Barbara Nathan—This easy-to-read, highly informative book is the definitive guide to basketball betting. Expert sports handicapper Barbara Nathan provides handicapping knowledge, insightful coverage, and step-by-step guidance for money management. The advantages and disadvantages of relying on sports services are also covered.
Softbound. $5.95. (ISBN: 0-89746-023-5)

The Gambling Times Guide to Football Handicapping by Bob McCune—Starting with the novice's approach to handicapping football, and winding up with some of the more sophisticated team selection techniques in the sports handicapping realm, this book will actually tell the reader how to forecast, *in advance,* the final scores of most major national football games. The author's background and expertise on the subject will put money into any sports gambler's pocket.
Softbound. $5.95. (ISBN: 0-89746-022-7)

The Gambling Times Guide to Greyhound Racing by William E. McBride—This complete discussion of greyhound racing is a must for

anyone who is just beginning to appreciate this exciting and profitable sport. The book begins with a brief overview detailing the origins of greyhound racing and pari-mutuel betting, and explains the greyhound track environment, betting procedures, and handicapping methods. Includes an appendix of various greyhound organizations, a review of greyhound books, and an interesting section on famous dogs and personalities in the world of greyhound racing.
Softbound. $5.95. (ISBN: 0-89746-007-3)

The Gambling Times Guide to Harness Racing by Igor Kusyshyn, Ph.D., Al Stanley and Sam Dragich—Three of Canada's top harness handicapping authorities present their inside approach to analyzing the harness racing scene and selecting winners. All the important factors from the type of sulky, workouts, drivers' ratings, speed, pace, etc., are skillfully presented in simple terms that can be used by novices and experienced racegoers to find the likely winners.
Softbound. $5.95. (ISBN: 0-89746-002-2)

The Gambling Times Guide to Jai Alai by William R. Keevers—The most comprehensive book on jai alai available. Author Bill Keevers takes the reader on an informative journey from the ancient beginnings of the game to its current popularity. This easy-to-understand guide will show you the fine points of the game, how to improve your betting percentage, and where to find jai alai frontons.
Softbound. $5.95. (ISBN: 0-89746-010-3)

The Gambling Times Guide to Thoroughbred Racing by R.G. Denis— Newcomers to the racetrack and veterans alike will appreciate the informative description of the thoroughbred pari-mutuel activity supplied by this experienced racing authority. Activities at the track and available information are blended skillfully in this guide to selecting winners that pay off in big-ticket returns.
Softbound. $5.95. (ISBN: 0-89746-005-7)

UPCOMING *GAMBLING TIMES* BOOKS

The following books will be at your local bookstore by September, 1984. If you can't find them there, they may also be ordered directly from *Gambling Times*.

Poker Books

Caro's Poker Encyclopedia by Mike Caro—Features alphabetical definitions and discussions of poker terms. Extensively cross-indexed, it can be used as a reference book to look up important poker terms (ante, bluff, sandbag) or it can be pleasurably read straight through. The definitions are brief; the advice is in-depth.
Softbound. $8.95. (ISBN: 0-89746-039-1)

Free Money: How to Win in the Cardrooms of California by Michael Wiesenberg—Computer expert and poker writer par excellence, Michael Wiesenberg delivers critical knowledge to those who play in the poker rooms of the western states. Wiesenberg gives you the precise meaning of the rules as well as the mathematics of poker to aid public and private poker players alike. Wiesenberg, a prolific author, is published by more gaming periodicals than any other writer.
Softbound. $6.95. (ISBN: 0-89746-027-8)

New Poker Games by Mike Caro—Features descriptions and winning strategies for well-thought-out but never-before-introduced forms of poker. Caro has already created two games: Caro Dots (through *Gambling Times*) and Tic Tac Hold 'Em. Tic Tac Hold 'Em was launched via a tournament held at the Imperial Palace in Las Vegas. While anyone can devise a new form of poker, few games are logically balanced. If a game isn't fine-tuned, illogical sequences of betting may occur, making the game strategically weak. Here is a collection of brand new games to liven up your next Friday night sessions.
Softbound. $5.95. (ISBN: 0-89746-040-5)

PROfile: The World's Greatest Poker Players by Stuart Jacobs—From background information, to style of play and ratings, this book adds personal interviews with all the poker greats, from the Grand Old Man of Poker, Johnny Moss, to the top women players like Betty Carey. If you

want to play like them, you'll need to read this book. If you want to play against them, you'd better read this book . . . first.
Hardbound. $15.00. (ISBN: 0-914314-05-X)

The Railbird by Rex Jones—The ultimate kibitzer, the man who watches from the rail in the poker room, has unique insights into the character and performance of all poker players. From this vantage point, Rex Jones, Ph.D., blends his expertise and considerable education in anthropology with his lifetime of poker playing and watching. The result is a delightful book with exceptional values for those who want to avoid the fatal errors of bad players and capitalize upon the qualities that make up the winning strengths of outstanding poker players.
Softbound. $6.95. (ISBN: 0-89746-028-6)

Tales Out of Tulsa by Bobby Baldwin—Oklahoma-born Bobby Baldwin, the youngest player to ever win the World Championship of Poker, is considered to be among the top five poker players in the world. Known affectionately as "The Owl," this brilliant poker genius, wise beyond his years, brings the benefits of his experience to the pages of this book. It's sure to stop the leaks in your poker game, and you will be amazingly ahead of your opponents in the very next game you play.
Softbound. $6.95. (ISBN: 0-89746-006-5)

World Class Poker, Play by Play by Mike Caro—Once again, Caro brings the world of poker to life. This time he gives us a one-card-at-a-time analysis of world class poker, with many card illustrations. This book includes discussions of professional tactics, then simulates game situations and asks the reader to make decisions. Next, Caro provides the answer and the hand continues. This learn-while-you-pretend-to-play format is a favorite teaching method of Caro's and one which meets with a great deal of success.
Hardbound. $20.00. (ISBN: 0-914314-06-08)

General Interest Books

Caro on Computer Gambling by Mike Caro—Caro discusses computers and how they will change gambling. He provides winning systems and descriptions of actual programs. This book will give the novice a taste of how computers work. Using the Pascal programming language, Caro

builds a working program step-by-step to show how a computer thinks and, also, how a human should analyze gambling propositions. This book is only slightly technical and mostly logical. Also discussed are ways that computers can cheat and speculation on the future of computers in gambling. Will you be able to type in your horse bets from your home computer? Can that personal computer be linked by phone into a perpetual poker game with the pots going straight into your bank account? The answers to these questions are found right here in Caro's book.
Softbound. $6.95. (ISBN: 0-89746-042-1)

The Casinos of the Caribbean by Stanley Roberts—The ultimate coffee-table book, in full color, showing the exotic vacation resorts of the Caribbean. Emphasis is placed on the casino activity on each island, with travel information, gaming advice and important shopping tips. As lush as the region it depicts, this volume will be the envy of your guests. Hardbound. $25.00. (ISBN: 0-914314-09-2)

The Casino Gourmet: Great Recipes from the Master Chefs of . . . by Stanley Roberts—This unique six-volume set showcases the top hotel restaurants in the resort areas of Las Vegas, Atlantic City, Reno/Lake Tahoe, the Caribbean, Europe and the Orient. For each restaurant, complete meals are featured, with recipes for the entrees and "Chef's Suggestions" for every appropriate item from appetizer to dessert. Comparable to classic coffee-table art books, each volume features color photographs of the hotels, casinos and restaurants.

The Casino Gourmet: Great Recipes from the Master Chefs of Las Vegas. Hardbound. $20.00. (ISBN: 0-914314-10-6)

The Casino Gourmet: Great Recipes from the Master Chefs of Atlantic City. Hardbound. $20.00. (ISBN: 0-914314-11-4)

The Casino Gourmet: Great Recipes from the Master Chefs of Reno/Lake Tahoe. Hardbound. $20.00. (ISBN: 0-914314-12-2)

The Casino Gourmet: Great Recipes from the Master Chefs of the Caribbean. Hardbound. $20.00. (ISBN: 0-914314-13-0)

The Casino Gourmet: Great Recipes from the Master Chefs of Europe. Hardbound. $20.00. (ISBN: 0-914314-14-9)

The Casino Gourmet: Great Recipes from the Master Chefs of the Orient. Hardbound. $20.00. (ISBN: 0-914314-15-7)

A Gambler's View of History by Mike Caro—Who was drawn out on, who made bad bets but then got lucky, and who was bluffed out in world affairs. Fun reading. Along the way, the reader may get some insights into how gambling tactics affect everyday, real-life decisions. It's Caro's contention that any world leader who truly understands probability has a much better chance of success. Unfortunately, leaders find themselves faced with once-in-a-lifetime situations. In these, they can easily make the correct decision and still meet disaster. Caro calls that "the equivalent of raising with a full house before the draw, but being unable to prevent an opponent from making a straight flush." Sometimes historic figures looked good even though they made wrong decisions; sometimes these historic figures made all the right decisions but did not look good. In this book, Caro explores the "whys and wherefores" of this seeming paradox.
Softbound. $7.95. (ISBN: 0-89746-043-X)

Gambling Greats: Profiles of the World's Greatest Gamblers by Pamela Shandel—From the legendary "Titanic" Thompson and Nick "The Greek" Dandelos, to the current heroes of the gambling scene such as Ed Thorp, Ken Uston and Stanley Roberts at blackjack; Johnny Moss, Doyle Brunson, Stu Ungar at poker; and a host of top backgammon, gin rummy and other gambling superstars, author Pamela Shandel details the lives, skills and significant events that make up the lore of gambling.
Hardbound. $14.00. (ISBN: 0-914314-16-5)

The Gambling Times Quiz Book by Mike Caro—Learn while testing your knowledge. Caro's book includes questions and answers on the concepts and information published in previous issues of *Gambling Times*. Caro tells why an answer is correct and credit is given to the author whose *Gambling Times* article suggested the question. This book covers only established fact, not the personal opinions of authors, and Caro's inimitable style makes this an easy-reading, easy-learning book.
Softbound. $5.95. (ISBN: 0-89746-031-6)

How the Superstars Gamble by Ron Delpit—Follow the stars to the racetracks, ball games, casinos and private clubs. You'll be amazed at how involved these world famous personalities are in the gambling scene, and how clever they are at the games they play. Ron Delpit, lifelong horse racing fan and confidant of innumerable showbiz greats, tells you fascinating tales about his friends, the superstars, with startling heretofore secret facts.
Hardbound. $12.00. (ISBN: 0-914314-17-3)

How to Win at Gaming Tournaments by Haven Earle Haley—Win your share of the millions of dollars and fabulous prizes being awarded to gaming contestants, and have the glory of being a World Champion. Poker, gin rummy, backgammon, craps, blackjack and baccarat are all popular tournament games. The rules, special tournament regulations, playing procedures, and how to obtain free entry are fully explained in this informative manual. The tournament promoters—who they are, where they hold events—and the cash and prizes awarded are explained in detail. Tournament play usually requires special strategy changes, which are detailed in this book.
Softbound. $8.95. (ISBN: 0-89746-016-2)

You're Comped: How to Be a Casino Guest by Len Miller—If you're a player you don't have to pay! Learn how to be "comped" in luxury casino-resort hotels the world over. A list of casinos together with names and addresses of junket representatives are included in this revealing guidebook. How to handle yourself on a junket is important if you want to receive all that you've been promised and be invited back again. How to do this, along with what you can expect from the casino, is explained in detail.
Softbound. $7.95. (ISBN: 0-89746-041-3)

Sports Betting Books

Cramer on Harness Race Handicapping by Mark Cramer—This systematic analysis of nuances in past performances will uncover patterns of improvement which will lead to flat bet profits. This book provides a functioning balance between creative handicapping and mechanical application.
Softbound. $6.95. (ISBN: 0-89746-026-X)

Cramer on Thoroughbred Handicapping by Mark Cramer—A unique approach to selecting winners, with price in mind, by distinguishing between valuable and common-place information. Results: higher average pay-offs and solid flat bet profits. How to spot signs of improvement and when to cash in. And much, much more.
Softbound. $6.95. (ISBN: 0-89746-025-1)

Ordering Information
Send your book order along with your check or money order to:

Gambling Times
1018 N. Cole Ave.
Hollywood, CA 90038

Softbound Books: Please add $1.00 per book if delivered in the United States, $1.50 in Canada or Mexico, and $3.50 for foreign countries.

Hardbound Books: Shipping charges for the following books are $2.50 if delivered in the United States, $3.00 in Canada or Mexico, and $5.00 for foreign countries:

According to Gambling Times: The Rules of Gambling Games
Caro's Book of Tells
The Casino Gourmet: Great Recipes from the Master Chefs of Atlantic City
The Casino Gourmet: Great Recipes from the Master Chefs of the Carribean
The Casino Gourmet: Great Recipes from the Master Chefs of Europe
The Casino Gourmet: Great Recipes from the Master Chefs of Las Vegas
The Casino Gourmet: Great Recipes from the Master Chefs of the Orient
The Casino Gourmet: Great Recipes from the Master Chefs of Reno/Lake Tahoe
The Casinos of the Carribean
Gambling Greats: Profiles of the World's Greatest Gamblers
How the Superstars Gamble
Million Dollar Blackjack
PROfile: The World's Greatest Poker Players
P$yching Out Vegas
World Class Poker, Play by Play